NATIONAL INSTITUTE FOR SOCIAL WORK TRAINING SERIES,
NO. 4

SOCIAL WORK WITH FAMILIES
READINGS IN SOCIAL WORK
VOLUME I

Publications by the
National Institute for Social Work Training
Mary Ward House, London, W.C.1
England

NO. 1. SOCIAL WORK AND SOCIAL CHANGE
by Eileen Younghusband

NO. 2. INTRODUCTION TO A SOCIAL WORKER
produced by the National Institute
for Social Work Training

NO. 3. SOCIAL POLICY AND ADMINISTRATION
by David Donnison

INTERVIEWING IN THE SOCIAL SERVICES
by Karl and Beth de Schweinitz

SOCIAL WORK WITH FAMILIES

READINGS IN SOCIAL WORK

VOLUME I

COMPILED BY

EILEEN YOUNGHUSBAND

D.B.E. LL.D., J.P.

London

GEORGE ALLEN & UNWIN LTD

RUSKIN HOUSE · MUSEUM STREET

FIRST PUBLISHED IN 1965

© *George Allen & Unwin Ltd, 1965*

PRINTED IN GREAT BRITAIN
in 11 on 12 point Fournier type
BY C. TINLING AND CO. LTD
LIVERPOOL, LONDON AND PRESCOT

PREFACE

This volume is the first in a series intended to preserve in more permanent form some of the most valuable articles which have appeared in British and American social work journals in the last few years. There are certain articles which are widely used and quoted, which have indeed become standard works but are not always easily available to busy social workers. The aim of the present series is thus twofold, both to preserve such articles and make them more widely available and at the same time by combining together the best that has been written on a given theme by social workers on both sides of the Atlantic to draw attention to recent developments in thought and knowledge.

The present volume represents current attempts by social workers to understand family interaction and to use this insight for family diagnosis and treatment. It illustrates a swing away from concentration on the individual towards the new concepts about the inter-relations between marriage partners, parents and children which are leading to significant advances in methods of study and treatment in family failure. Several authors also analyse the range of behaviour which is 'normal' or pathological in various family and social situations.

It is hoped that this collection of articles will be widely used by practising social workers, by social teachers and by students not only in Great Britain and the United States but in those many other parts of the world where the profession of social work is advancing towards higher standards of practice.

The National Institute for Social Work Training has received much helpful co-operation from the authors of the articles which form this book and from the journals in which they appeared. In addition to expressing our indebtedness to the authors the following acknowledgments are made with gratitude to the journals in which the articles originally appeared:

The Almoner (London) for permission to reprint 'Notes on the Role Concept in Casework with Mothers of Burned Children'; *The British Journal of Psychiatric Social Work* published by the Association of Psychiatric Social Workers, London, for permission to reprint 'David and His Mother'; *Case Conference* (London) for permission to reprint 'Children's Play as a Concern of Family Caseworkers and Children at Risk'; *The Family Discussion Bureau*, The Tavistock Institute of Human

Relations, London, for permission to reprint 'The Nature of Marital Interaction'; *Social Casework* (New York) for permission to reprint 'Concepts Relevant to Helping the Family as a Group', 'Chronic Sorrow: A Response to Having a Mentally Defective Child', 'Family Diagnosis: Trends in Theory and Practice' and 'Designing an Instrument to Assess Parental Coping Mechanisms', with the permission of the Family Service Association of America, New York; *The Social Service Review* published by the University of Chicago Press, Chicago, Illinois, for permission to reprint 'Helping a Child Adapt to Stress: The Use of Ego Psychology in Casework' (Copyright 1957 by the University of Chicago), 'A Family Diagnosis Model' and 'Applying Family Diagnosis in Practice' (both copyright 1960 by The University of Chicago); *Social Work* (London) for permission to reprint 'The Normal Family—Myth and Reality'; *Social Work* (New York) for permission to reprint 'Treatment in the Home and Social Determinants of Family Behavior', with the permission of The National Association of Social Workers, New York.

CONTENTS

———————

CONTENTS

1

THE NORMAL FAMILY—MYTH AND REALITY*

E. M. GOLDBERG

As social workers we mostly meet families in trouble. Chronic illness may have disrupted their accustomed ways of living, delinquency, marital unhappiness and many other disturbances in personal relationships are rife among such families. When trying to help, consciously or unconsciously we carry in our mind some image, some 'norm' as to what ordinary healthy family life is or should be like. Without these implicit assumptions and rough guides, we could not make any assessments, or have a positive aim. Some colleagues will throw up their hands in horror at the suggestion that we have 'norms', values or a philosophy of life that inspires our work and gives it direction. They will say that it is our job to try to understand each family's unique needs and difficulties in relation to their life experiences and their social setting as objectively as possible and that help will aim at solutions which are appropriate to the clients' special situations; that our own values, judgment and ideals do not enter into the situation, and that we do not try to get our clients to conform to what *we* perceive to be the 'good' or 'healthy' life, but to the standards that are 'good' or 'healthy' for *them*. These colleagues will point out that the 'moralistic' kind of social work was done by our forebears whose religious and moral values permeated their activities and who had a clear vision of the good life which they helped their more unfortunate brethren and sisters to achieve; they sought to uplift them.

Sometimes I envy these early pioneers who carried their values and ideals openly and proudly, who knew where they wanted to go and where they wanted their clients to go. We, social workers of today, on the other hand, may or may not hold certain religious, moral and social values. At any rate we claim that we do not impose them on our

* Published in *Social Work* (London), Vol. XVI, No. 1, January 1959.

clients, whose troubles we try to disentangle with them, leaving them free to choose the end to which they would put these insights. However, I suggest that in the last resort we have to make up our minds what we consider to be healthy or unhealthy, good or bad in family life and in social life generally. We now hide our value judgments behind such terms as 'well-functioning' and 'poorly-functioning' families, 'mature' and 'immature' individuals, and so on. But well-functioning and poorly-functioning, mature and immature by what standards? If we examine these concepts of social health and disease, we find that they are closely bound up with the social values of the society, the social class, the 'sub culture' to which we belong, and that what we call social or mental health is not based on objective universal or absolute criteria. It seems to me that the clinicians, the child guidance workers, the caseworkers have an ideal family in mind when they make their assessments, when they say that this mother is 'over-protective', and that father 'authoritarian'. The ideal 'child-guidance-social-case-work, progressive-psychology' kind of family is vividly described by Seeley, *et al* in their study of a Canadian middle class community, highly conscious of the need for 'good mental health', called *Crestwood Heights*.

' "Good" parents are emotionally secure, free from hyper-anxiety, and from covert or overt conflict with persons in their immediate environment . . .

'The good mother must not be over-solicitous or over-protective. She must be undisturbed by worries about the future, confident in her status and in her acceptance by the community, and sure of her adequacy in the fulfilment of her maternal role. She should not find it necessary to translate any anxieties she may have into specific worries about the child's health, safety, or ability to measure up to academic or social expectations, particularly in the school setting. The ideal mother is not "over-dominant"—an attitude manifested in nagging or "bossing" the child. She is neither over-permissive nor inconsistent in discipline; nor does she cater to the child's every whim.

'The good father also exhibits these characteristics (although most discussion of parental behaviour seems to refer to mothers). But in avoiding the Scylla of "authoritarianism", the good father must not run against the Charybdis of "indulgence". The Victorian father, patriarchal head of the family and owner of wife and progeny, is as frowned upon as the "over-dominant" and nagging mother . . .

' "Unconditional" parental affection and acceptance, where the child is concerned, has now become the central ideal . . .

'Conflict between mother and son, mother and daughter, father and son, father and daughter, is regarded as a symptom of family malfunction . . .'[1]

Incidentally, the mental health of the Crestwood Heights children growing up in families inspired by these ideals of maturity, democracy, and integration of relationships, was no better, in fact possibly less good, than that of children growing up under what might be thought far less favourable conditions.

It seems desirable then to take a closer look at some of the rough working hypotheses on which consciously or unconsciously we base our evaluations and casework help.

I want to do this in two ways. First, I would like to refer briefly to recent family studies which have scrutinized carefully some common and fairly sweeping assumptions about the modern normal family. Secondly, I want to discuss in greater detail the family relationships among so-called normal families which I have come across.

One assumption which is repeatedly made is that the modern urban family is isolated, that is to say that they live far away from their extended kin, for instance from the husband's and wife's parents and from their brothers and sisters. It is often suggested that the modern young mother is lonely and receives no help from her relatives. Yet studies of working class families in two London boroughs, one East and one West[2] have shown in a vivid and convincing way that the three-generation family is still very much with us; that there is a close link, especially between married daughters and their mothers, but also between married men and their mothers. Grandmothers continue to be a great standby in crises of all kinds and in the daily round of living, particularly as regards the children. These are not impressions but facts which have been patiently collected from an unselected sample in a defined population. For instance 66 per cent of the men and 81 per cent of the women in the Bethnal Green sample, who had mothers alive, had seen them during the week preceding the interview. In these old-established working class areas the nuclear family, far from being isolated, is embedded in a close network of family and neighbourly relations, the ideal being that once married one should live *near* but not *with* one's parents. It has also been shown that it is the housing

[1] John R. Seeley, R. A. Sim and E. W. Looseley, *Crestwood Heights*, Constable & Co., London, 1956, pp. 165, 166.
[2] Michael Young and Peter Willmott, *Family and Kinship in East London*, Routledge & Kegan Paul, London, 1957.
L. A. Shaw, 'Impressions of Family Life in a London Suburb', *Sociological Review*, Vol. II, No. 2, 1954.

policies of authorities, national and local, rather than changing social values in the local community itself which tend to break up these extended family ties. These studies which demonstrate the vital importance of the maternal grandmother in working class family life and in the upbringing of children, are of immediate relevance to family caseworkers who, largely under the influence of modern psychology, have concentrated perhaps too exclusively on the relationships within the nuclear family. However, Young, Wilmott and Shaw worked in homogeneous working class districts; what about the lower middle class or middle class families? Are they not isolated, as they have often moved around a good deal to better jobs for example, or to better neighbourhoods? Elizabeth Bott in her studies of ordinary families[1] which included a high proportion of middle class ones, has given some suggestive answers. The urban middle class families, were surrounded by what she called a 'loosely knit network' of relationships, relatives and friends who might be scattered and not know each other, rather than by a closely knit network like the families in Bethnal Green where relatives and friends all knew each other. Thus these urban families were not more isolated but more 'individuated' than families in relatively small closed communities.

Elizabeth Bott has also thrown light on another assumption social workers often make in evaluating the stability or goodness of a marital relationship. We seem to suppose that the good and happy marriage is based on a close partnership in which interests are shared, problems discussed, and roles flexible and interchangeable. There is of course little doubt that generally speaking the emancipation of women has made marriage much more of an equal partnership. But how true is the assumption that the more joint and interchangeable the roles of husband and wife are and the more interests they share, the better for them and their children?

Both Bott and Young found that if husband and wife come from close knit family networks like those prevalent in Bethnal Green and if they can remain in touch with this network of kin and friends after marriage, then the marriage is superimposed on the previous relationships and each partner continues to be drawn into activities with outside people. 'Each gets some satisfaction from these external relationships and demands correspondingly less from the spouse. Rigid segregation of conjugal roles is possible because each partner can get help from people outside, but if husband and wife come to marriage with loose knit networks, or if their networks become loose knit after

[1] Elizabeth Bott, *Family and Social Network*, Tavistock Publications, London, 1957.

marriage, they must seek in each other some of the emotional satisfaction and help with familiar tasks that couples in close knit networks can get from outsiders. Joint organization becomes more necessary for the success of the family as an enterprise.'[1] Both these investigators have shown us that marriages in which conjugal roles are segregated where the husband goes to the pub regularly, attends his clubs, goes fishing with his pals and where the wife does all the housework and the washing up goes round to mum's frequently and maintains close relationships with female neighbours, are no less happy or conducive to bringing up happy children than those marriages with more joint activities and sharing of roles.

I became acutely aware of my own false assumptions about joint partnership being the prerequisite to a happy family life when I found that among 64 couples of fairly ordinary families in a working class area, only a handful of wives shared their husband's interests. The wives considered the husband's hobbies and interests to belong to a separate male world rather like his occupation.

What matters most is probably whether the role assignments really suit both partners' needs and conform to the social norms of their group. Indeed, research into the more psychological aspects of closely joint and segregated types of role relationships between parents, may indicate that it is easier for the child to identify with the parent of his own sex if the roles are clearly distinguishable and thus provide recognizable models.

Yet another assumption which is often made about family life is that families can only function well and children thrive if mothers stay at home and do not go out to work. Working mothers have been blamed for the rise in juvenile delinquency, for disturbed and backward children, and for unruly adolescents. It is a subject highly charged with emotion and peculiarly void of facts. Do we know from unbiased studies whether the children of women who go out to work are less healthy or more disturbed than those of mothers who stay at home? For instance comparisons could be made between groups of children whose mothers go out to work and those who stay at home, in terms of their health records, school achievements, absences from school, delinquency rates and general social adjustment. Do we know whether children living in extended families fare better when their mothers go out to work than children living in relatively isolated nuclear families? More intensive clinical studies could test the hypothesis that the consequences for the family, and for the children in particular, differ with

[1] Ibid., p. 60.

the life experiences and motives that impel the mother to go out to work, as well as with the mother's capacities to handle the double job and the support she gets from her husband. Some studies are now in progress. A follow up study of children from all parts of Great Britain and all social classes born in 1946 is being carried out and results have so far been published up to the age of five.[1] So far there are no differences between the children of working and non-working mothers as regards their heights, frequency of accidents and emotional disturbances, but the investigation continues and differences may yet emerge at a later stage of the children's development. Another study was carried out by the London School of Economics in South London among mothers who do the 'double job' and those who stay at home. The findings did not suggest that mothers who go out to work neglect their families or that their homes and children suffered; on the contrary they were on the whole more capable mothers and housewives than their counterparts who did not go out to work.[2]

In my own work among one group of families containing a son with a psychosomatic illness and a group of ordinary families with a healthy son, there was a hint which gainsaid the assumption that it is harmful for mothers of young children to go out to work. The mothers of the healthy young men had gone out to work much more often during the first ten years of their son's lives than the mothers of the sick sons. The mothers of the sons with the psychosomatic illness were as a rule capable, intelligent women full of energy and drive who had followed their consciences to stay at home and be 'good mothers' and at times they appeared to have looked after their children almost too well. The mothers of the healthy young men on the other hand had been more easy going and possibly less conscientious in the care of their children but they had been more flexible with more diverse interests that took them outside their homes and enabled them to combine work with family life and consequently to make fewer emotional demands on their children.

It is all the more important to find out what the effect of mothers working is on family life for as the *Manchester Guardian* reminded us some time ago (January 13, 1958) the spinster, the unmarried professional woman who has manned the nursing, social and teaching services will be fast disappearing. The Report of the Royal Commission on Population, calculated that by 1962 there will be equal

[1] J. W. B. Douglas and J. H. Blomfield, *Children Under Five*, Allen & Unwin, London 1958.
[2] Pearl Jephcott (with Nancy Seear and John H. Smith), *Married Women Working*, Allen & Unwin, London, 1962.

numbers of men and women and by 1972 there will be a small excess of men.[1] Unless we can think of the normal family as one in which mothers go out to work when their children begin to grow up, we may see many of the traditional women's occupations denuded of personnel unless of course the 'surplus' bachelors were to take over. Myrdal and Klein[2] have pointed out that before the industrial revolution removed many of the economic functions of the family into factories, women were always used to a double role, that of home maker and worker, but with the important difference that the work was carried on at home.

Finally I want to compare the implicit assumptions we make about normal family life with a few examples of so-called normal families I have come across. These normal families are part of a control group in a study concerned with psychosomatic illness. They were drawn from the register of a general practitioner. Readers will ask, did not these ordinary families resent this intrusion? Did they talk frankly to you? Can you really expect them to reveal anything about themselves if they have not asked for any help? These are important questions which I have considered in other contexts.[3] Here I can only mention briefly that in this study, as in others, the assumption that British people in contrast to Americans are reticent and will not talk about themselves has been proved wrong. Three-quarters of the families approached co-operated straight away. There were refusals of course and these are of great interest. For, again contrary to the common assumption that it is the odd people who co-operate and like to display themselves and the normal ones who refuse, it appeared that the unco-operative families had more serious problems than the families who did co-operate. It seemed that families need to feel a certain amount of confidence in their ability to cope with life reasonably well and in their own 'goodness' before they can entrust their experiences to the scrutiny of a stranger, however understanding.

Thirty-two normal families were studied by interviews at home and at the research unit, and in this article I can only touch on the kind of psychological and social adjustments found in some marital relationships. The most striking impression I carried away with me from the investigation was the great variety of ways in which people can relate

[1] *Report of the Royal Commission on Population*, H.M.S.O. London, 1949.
[2] A. Myrdal and V. Klein, *Women's Two Roles: Home and Work*, Routledge & Kegan Paul, London, 1956.
[3] E. M. Goldberg, 'Experiences of Families of Young Men with Duodenal Ulcer' and ' "Normal" Control Families: Some Problems of Approach and Method', *British Journal of Medical Psychology*, Vol. XXVI, Pts. 3 and 4, 1953. *Family Influences and Psychosomatic Illness*, Tavistock Publications, London, 1958.

B

to one another and be reasonably happy, and how unlike the child guidance stereotype of the well-adjusted family these adaptations really were.

Mr and Mrs Hodges were a striking example of a couple who had assumed roles that fitted in with their mutual needs although these roles were not modelled on the conventional notions of the man doing the work outside and the wife keeping the home.

The wife, a very intelligent, capable, and somewhat excitable woman, was the daughter of a strict Victorian widow. During her childhood she had had to work hard scrubbing and sewing while her mother and younger brother went out to enjoy themselves. When her brother was killed in World War I, her mother said, 'Why couldn't it have been you?' Mr Hodges was a highly intelligent, sensitive, contemplative type of man of considerable maturity. His wife 'played him up terrifically' during their courtship because she said she could not believe that anyone wanted her for herself. She refused to marry until Mr Hodges could offer her a home, as she did not want him to live in her mother's house. (This behaviour may have indicated a fear that the situation would be re-created in which the maternal grandmother would prefer the man in the house, and put Mrs Hodges into an inferior position.) In her marriage she took over the leadership, if only by virtue of her tremendous energy and vitality, which at times seemed inexhaustible to Mr Hodges. She seemed unable to relax and at the age of fifty was doing a full-time job, as well as a considerable amount of private dressmaking, and her home always looked neat and tidy. It seemed as though her unremitting activity still represented an unconscious response to her mother's admonition to work hard.

Mr Hodges, on the other hand, was a quiet person who could relax easily and who liked the peace and quiet of the countryside. Although he often discussed the futility of her continual drive and activity and still tried to persuade her to adopt a more relaxed way of living, he had in fact accepted her as she was, and they had worked out many compromise solutions to suit each other's temperaments. Mrs Hodges often spent Sunday washing and sewing and sent her husband out on a bicycle ride in the country. Another week-end she would be equally ready to leave her work and go on an excursion with him. One Sunday they would do something that suited the husband's taste—a walk in the country—and another Sunday they would go on a more hectic and exciting expedition into town, which suited Mrs Hodges.

These adjustments were not reached without a struggle. It looked as though Mrs Hodges had worked through many of her childhood problems in the course of her married life, her husband being the ever-kind, helpful, mature person who could respond to her needs. At first she played her husband up as though to test him. Then for many years she appeared to have turns of psychosomatic or nervous illness. She would keep well for about nine months and collapse into dependence and helplessness for about three months when Mr Hodges would nurse her. He spoke with satisfaction and without any trace of resentment about his nursing role as though it fulfilled a need in him. After her menopause Mrs Hodges lost these nervous symptoms, and during the last ten years has been fitter than ever before. However, she still continued to drive herself until she almost collapsed and could do no more. At this point she would retire to bed and her husband would bring her cocoa and look after her. This couple recognized that they were reversing some of the conventional male and female roles. Mr Hodges mentioned that his colleagues at work were amazed at the freedom he granted his wife, for example letting her go to dances without him. On the other hand, he did a good deal of the housework. When his wife sat at the sewing-machine wanting to get something finished, the only way to get his tea was to make it himself. Mrs Hodges on her side said quite openly that she did not like housework and preferred machining. They thought that many of the accepted roles were conventions and that they were happy doing things their way.

Each felt a deep affection for the other, and they discussed their experiences with animation, neither of them being afraid to voice their opinion, even at the risk of an argument. Seen together, they showed many indications that their differences in temperament were a source of struggle as well as satisfaction. They had quite heated arguments about the wife's insistence on doing the washing at the week-ends, and about her excessive work. Yet, the wife's initiative and daring aroused great admiration in the husband, who by contrast considered himself a rather 'dull, routine chap'. Recently she had started to play the violin and attempted to learn to ride a motor bicycle. Mrs Hodges, though occasionally exasperated by his placidity, loved the gentle and mature stability of her husband, which presumably symbolized for her a combination of a father she never had and of a gentle, loving mother who would comfort her when she could go on no longer. Their aspirations and values were another important bond between them. In many discussions they tried to work out their aims in the up-bringing of their children and other basic problems of living.

How did the children fare in such a marriage? There were two sons—complete opposites in their emotional make-up and behaviour. The older was a highly intelligent, studious young man, very quiet and reserved who concealed his feelings; 'he thinks rather than speaks.' He distinguished himself at school and in the army, and made rapid progress in his engineering job, acquiring additional qualifications at evening classes. He had married an intelligent but rather slovenly wife (a great contrast to his mother), and had two children. He had never presented any problem to his parents, except that he showed a marked reserve especially towards his mother, having been very closely attached to his maternal grandmother in his early years. Peter, the younger brother, was 'a duffer at school', inattentive and a scatter-brain. He was closely attached to his mother. He was full of explosive feeling, had a lively imagination and a great need to communicate. One of his emotional outlets was his violin, which he played beauti-fully. He was very active, clever with his hands, had a great zest for life, a love of speed and went in for cycle racing. The days never seemed long enough for all his activities. Many of these characteristics were strongly reminiscent of his mother. As a child he had had many fears and accidents and was quite unable to tolerate evacuation. At the age of twenty-three he was settling down to a job in steel erecting in which he could indulge his love of hard work and his daring. He had loosened his tight bonds to his mother and was working away from home most of the time, reserving a warm communicative and trusting relationship with both parents.

Here we see two contrasting ways of adapting to a strong and powerful mother—by withdrawal and reserve, and by strong identi-fication. Although Mrs Hodges could be called a neurotic and dominant mother and although these characteristics left their mark on both children, the family was a happy cohesive one in which the children were able to develop their potentialities. This was made possible by Mrs Hodges marrying a mature man with complementary needs and qualities to hers who provided a strong positive and stabilizing force, not only for her but for the family in general.

Another example of a complementary marriage which was satisfying to both partners, although it may have been built on mutual neurotic needs, was that of Mr and Mrs Bradshaw.

Mrs Bradshaw had lost her mother early in life, and was brought up by a very intelligent, successful, and possessive father, who expected her to wait on him and look after him as long as he lived. It never occurred to him that she might want to marry. When at work she had to give up all her earnings to him and hardly ever went out in the evenings. Although she resented these restrictions she was deeply devoted to her father and admired him greatly. Her husband courted her for many years. He had had a rough, deprived childhood, and was as dependent and ineffective as her father was dominating and successful. Finally, when she was in her early thirties she married him 'more out of pity than love', having made it quite clear to him that so long as her father was alive, he would come first. They lived in her father's house, and he continued to be the head of the household. Mrs Bradshaw, although she wanted a child, wondered whether it was right to embark on this, in case her father might feel jealous and pushed out of things. After her father's death, Mrs Bradshaw took over many of his roles. She became the 'man about the house' doing the plastering, the papering and the painting. Mr Bradshaw was not expected to help as he was not considered capable of 'driving a nail in straight'. Through the years he had a succession of illnesses: an ulcer, anaemia, bronchitis, followed by a great deal of invalidism. The panel doctor referred to him as a 'gross hysteric'. Mrs Bradshaw fulfilled the most exacting maternal and nursing functions for him cheerfully until he returned to work. At one time when he had to be at his job at 6 a.m., Mrs Bradshaw used to get up at 3.30 in order to get him ready for work and would then walk to the station with him. While she provided this maternal care for her husband, she also gradually built him up to take on her father's role of a tyrant who had to be waited on. Both she and her husband were aware of this development. The husband discussed how he would have been quite ready to get his own things or hang up his coat, for example, but his wife insisted on doing it for him. Although she never was 'in love' with this man they felt a great deal of affection for each other, and expressed it freely, Mrs Bradshaw saying that they were 'still like sweethearts'.

How did it come about that two such emotionally disabled people could give so much to each other? It seems that this immature, dependent man, who lacked maternal love in his childhood, had some of his needs fulfilled by this maternal self-sacrificing wife. She, in order to satisfy her needs, had to keep him a dependent child, thus preventing him from ever growing up emotionally. In this way she was able to serve her husband as she had served her father, working hard and never sparing herself in order to prove herself worthy of his love. (She had had a rival for her father's love in the form of a much more attractive sister.) The relationship also gave her a chance to identify with her father in becoming the superior man in the home who directed all activities from budgetting to plastering. It may rightly be said that both Mr and Mrs Bradshaw were emotionally sick. Mr Bradshaw was a hysteric and Mrs Bradshaw, who was frigid and masochistic, seemed to have considerable unresolved Oedipal problems. It could even be maintained that the relationship was a mutual acting out of their neuroses. But, although the marital relationship was determined by their childhood fixations, it provided substitute satisfactions for these childhood needs and enabled them to lead useful and even happy lives. It is questionable whether any psychiatric treatment of either individually could have done more to help them than the relationship they had worked out for themselves.

The Bradshaws had one son who turned out to be a healthy, well adjusted, and interesting young man, who derived much satisfaction from his job as a toolmaker, had many interests and hobbies and a wide circle of friends including girls, though he refused 'to go steady' yet at the age of twenty-four. His relationship with his mother was one of comradeship and sharing of ideas. He would discuss technicalities of his job with her, of which she showed an unusual grasp. He had a kindly tolerance for his father whom he considered to have no 'go' in him and with whom he shared much less than with his mother. There were indications, however, that during childhood the father was heeded and respected and that father and son had done things together.

Again it seems that the satisfying marital relationship was able to absorb the parents' neurotic and infantile needs which they did not have to project on to their child. They carried out their parental roles constructively. Their son considered that he had had a happy childhood. He felt neither constrained, over-protected, nor pushed out; he thought that he had had a reasonable amount of freedom, help and affection from his parents. Despite the neurotic disabilities of his parents he had developed into a stable, happy, outgoing man who was able to enjoy life and who was generous to his parents without feeling under any 'obligation' to them as the only child.

Mr and Mrs Brewer's marriage represented the kind of relationship in which contradictory aims are revealed. Frustrations were felt on both sides, but strong forces of affection were constantly at work to resolve their difficulties. This marriage was rated as a good one in spite of difficulties because of the positive feeling that led the father and the mother to 'please each other', as the son put it. Their choice can again be understood in terms of their childhood experiences. The mother was greatly attached to her father, a grocer, who had died suddenly when she was in her teens. She had then started to work as a cashier in another grocer's store where she had met Mr Brewer. He, like her father, was a grocer and was described by her as cheerful and easy-going—characteristics also reminiscent of her father. Mr Brewer, whose easy-going optimism and even temper were his outstanding qualities, came from a home where his father, a heavy drinker, was often unkind to his mother. He was intelligent and ambitious, and had become the manager of a shop at twenty-one, and had a great zest for adventure and change. It seemed that he chose a wife who could help him in his business, and provide an antidote for his somewhat impulsive and daring ways of conducting business. Whereas he took risks, Mrs Brewer was of a careful disposition; it was she who kept the books and maintained a close control over the financial situation. He exerted a strong influence on his two sons who looked upon him with great admiration and affection.

The husband had very definite ideas that the man should be the leader in the home. Mr Brewer would enjoy, as well as laugh at, his wife's way of waiting on him and the children, calling her a 'martyr who makes herself indispensable' by her constant services. His generosity—and possibly the memory of his father's unkindness to his mother—led him to lavish all the comforts he could think of on his wife. She was gratified by his gifts and said proudly that there was nothing she wanted that he would not give her. Indeed, the home contained all the up-to-date equipment one could wish for. Mrs Brewer had all the clothes she wanted and the smartest car in the neighbourhood. At the same time Mr Brewer felt a certain amount of resentment at his wife's 'martyrdom', which, he maintained, made him feel guilty, at her hoarding activities and her 'blooming houseproudness', and at her need to keep the children close to her. However, this resentment was voiced freely in front of her, and Mrs Brewer put up a fairly spirited defence, remarking on his helplessness in the home and on his untidiness, which she tried to tolerate. She readily admitted her problems over wanting to 'hang on to her children'. This kind of discussion did not appear to be unusual between this couple and they gave the impression that they were able to communicate their feelings and criticisms with comparative ease, and with an underlying feeling of confidence that their relationship could stand this kind of scrutiny. In the actual course of living together, they had evolved many compromises which allowed them both to satisfy some of their needs. The father was as dirty and messy as he liked in his workshop, and the mother was as clean and obsessional as she needed to be in the living rooms. Mr Brewer indulged in his relaxation of fishing, whereas Mrs Brewer liked to go to town and look at the shops.

But there were also many things they enjoyed doing together. They said that they enjoyed each other's company so much that they hardly ever felt the need to go out in the evenings and seek distraction or meet friends. They were trying to counteract this isolationist tendency by taking dancing lessons together so that they might enjoy dances and official functions more. As their sons were likely to leave home soon they were thinking of taking up golf. When a crisis occurred, as it did over their younger son's love affair, they tried to thrash things out and faced their differences in outlook, which led to heated clashes between them. These differences lay in the father's basic optimism and tendency to rush into things, and the mother's more rigid and cautious pessimism. Mr and Mrs Brewer had two sons, both healthy and reasonably stable lads, who joined the father in his business and Mrs Brewer helped with the book-keeping. They were a happy working community. The father was worried, however, lest he had protected his sons too much. 'They are not standing on their own feet but on my shoulders.' The mother missed them badly when they were away in the Forces, and wrote to them every night. When one of the sons was jilted, the family rallied round and he was able to join their activities for a while before he was ready to pick up with outside friends again. The family enjoyed doing things together, going on holiday or on week-end outings. It remains to be seen how the two sons will be able to emancipate themselves and build up a life of their own.

The Cox family presented another interesting example of many outward tensions between members who were basically bound together by strong ties of affection.

Mrs Cox was an obsessional woman who spent her life cleaning. She was married to an easy-going, untidy husband who strewed his ash all over the place and enjoyed sprawling in front of the fire at the weekend. He would have liked his wife to abandon all her housework then and share his pleasures with him. She, however, found this impossible and 'hoovered around him'. She was fully aware of his wishes but could not help herself. Yet her admiration for her husband was intense. 'If there is anything wrong with my husband it's me. He is the best, most wonderful man I can think of in this world and we are as much in love as ever.' She would talk of his generosity and thoughtfulness, and of the many ways in which they expressed their affection for each other. He, though exasperated by her cleaning orgies and restlessness, said that he would not change her for anything in the world.

The son was a studious undergraduate, something of an isolate, with many neurotic problems. He had had many battles with his mother from the time he was a toddler. He would argue with her and become exasperated by her 'ignorance'. He would play classical music, which she could not stand; he would refuse to do her shopping, yet after an argument he would pick up the shopping basket as though nothing had happened. Despite his criticism he was well aware of the positive elements in his home life. Thus on one occasion he compared himself with fellow-students living in a hostel and remarked how profoundly grateful he was to 'be able to put my feet on the mantelpiece and have nice food and comfort'. His sister, a little younger, was a lively girl, who worked in a factory and had a steady boy friend. She was extravagant and stubborn and had more sustained rows with her mother than did her brother. Brother and sister too would argue and tease each other, but when it came to any issues with the parents they would put up a united front. The mother had a tendency to identify herself with her children and derived much enjoyment through sharing their lives. She kept an open house, and the children's friends were entertained generously. The father, a steel-worker, who worked away from home most of the time, tended to be a little envious of his growing children and the fun they were having. There was rivalry between him and Cyril. If Cyril gave his mother a dozen tulips the father would appear a few days later with a bunch of tulips and a bunch of daffodils. He was also concerned over his daughter's late hours, although formerly he had encouraged his wife to give her more freedom. On the other hand, his generosity towards his children was remarkable.

The arguments and disagreements that were fought out in this family were numerous. The mother got exasperated about the way the family expected to be waited on. Cyril got annoyed with his mother's many attempts at telling him what to do. The mother often spoilt the father's pleasure by insisting on doing her housework, and then felt very guilty about it. The daughter had fights with her mother over quite unimportant issues which resulted in sulks on both sides lasting several days during which they would not speak to each other. They all were aware of these tensions and had a good appreciation of what the other member was feeling. They verbalized their feelings readily, were frankly critical of each other, and sparks flew easily. At the same time they all had a strong sense of humour which often helped them to regain a sense of proportion; they were all very generous and loved to give each other presents; and there was a strong feeling of solidarity between them. Major decisions were made by a 'family council'. They all had a considerable capacity for enjoying life and at Christmas the father could not do enough to make it a happy time for everyone. Their feeling of being a united family despite their many dissensions seemed to be conveyed when the father decided not to buy individual presents one Christmas, but a radiogram for them all.

What can be learned from this cursory look at the marital relationships in ordinary families who were functioning fairly adequately?

First, that they are not so different from the kinds of families we all know, both among our friends or our clients. In other words there is no sharp division between the normal and abnormal, but rather a spectrum and an almost infinite variety of combinations of attitudes within it. The variability within the normal has also become increasingly clear in the physiological field where many phenomena which used to be treated as pathological are now recognized to be variations within the norm. For instance some heart murmurs in children, certain kinds of blood pressure and minor orthopaedic disabilities which used to be treated with splints and exercises— incidentally causing a good deal of emotional disturbance.

Secondly, that neurotic symptoms, oddities, and unconventional role assignments need not necessarily lead to unhappy families or severely maladjusted children as long as the members of the family can play roles which help to fulfil their own as well as the needs of others in the family and as long as there is some capacity to tolerate individual differences and some sharing of common values. Only when emotional instability is combined with incompatability between the parents and conflicting values, does the family cohesion and the mental health of their members seem seriously threatened.

Finally, I hope that the stereotype of the mature democratic family is getting a little blurred and that instead readers may remember Mr Hodges making his tea while his wife is machining furiously, or going off in a huff on his bicycle with Peter on Sunday morning because Mrs Hodges is surrounded by washing yet again, or Mr Brewer coming up with filthy boots from his workshop to the gleaming sitting room which Mrs Brewer has already polished twice today. After a jolly good dig at each other they can be seen walking down the road arm-in-arm to the cinema; or one might still hear the uproar in the Cox family because Jean did not tell Mum that her water bottle had leaked, father laughing his head off, Cyril upholding mother and pointing reproachfully to the big stain in the beautiful new mattress and Jean stalking out of the place.

Some readers will now shrug their shoulders and conclude: 'There is no such thing as "normal", we are all crazy. Why bother?' This is not so. I would suggest the 'normal' or the well-functioning family does exist but that its normality consists in a tolerable 'fit' between what members of a family seek from each other and receive in return, and also perhaps in a fit between their values and ways of living and those of the social group or network to which they belong.

2

CONCEPTS RELEVANT TO HELPING THE FAMILY AS A GROUP*

GRACE LONGWELL COYLE

BOTH in casework practice and in recent theoretical articles in the professional literature, the family as a group has begun to emerge as the unit of casework treatment. This shift in focus requires, among other things, a framework of concepts about group behaviour and group dynamics which will be useful to the caseworker who is extending his helping efforts on behalf of the family.

The implications, for practice, of the use of group concepts as they may influence the conduct of group interviews on home visits, and other ways of diagnosing or treating the family as a whole, will not be considered here. I believe that it is the function of casework practitioners, rather than group workers, to determine the usefulness of such concepts and the precise ways in which they can be applied in the treatment of families. My intent is to discuss generic concepts, derived from the experience of group workers in serving groups, which may also be applicable to casework practice.

In its recent manifestations the emphasis placed on the family as a group has taken several forms. It is true, as many writers have indicated recently, that the family-centred focus was evident in Mary Richmond's writings and has remained a central element in family casework practice. It is equally true, however, that for a long period of time the dynamic concepts of human behaviour derived from psychiatry served to focus casework practice primarily on the individual and on his intrapsychic problems. Presumably, however, the individual was always viewed within the context of his social situation, and his family was regarded as the most important aspect of that situation. What, then, is the new element in what is called the family-centred approach, or the approach to the family as a group? As an

* Published in *Social Casework*, Vol. XLIII, No. 7, July, 1962.

outside observer I should like to venture the guess that three separate but simultaneous movements, or trends, are being classed together under the same name. Most of my discussion will be concerned with only one of these movements, but I should like first to place it in its larger setting.

The first of these movements is the increased emphasis on the relationships of an individual with other members of his immediate family. As one writer put it, 'The family is more than the sum of several different personalities; it is, in addition, the interaction of those personalities and their influence on each other'.[1] Although this statement seems to indicate a concept of the family as a whole, the predominant phenomenon referred to is the influence of family members on each other. In some instances, primary attention has been given to the mother-child relationship; in others, to the husband-wife relationship. With the growing recognition that practice as well as theory should accord the father a more significant place in the family constellation, even the father-child relationship has come in for greater attention. The same holds true for the relationship of a child to his siblings. The theory used to underpin this development is chiefly psychiatric and is concerned in large part with the intrapsychic elements in family relationships. So far as I have been able to discover, no additional concepts about the family as a group are used in this type of practice except as the significance of these intimate family relationships for each individual member is given greater importance and is more extensively explored by the practitioner.

The second movement that is proceeding simultaneously with the emphasis on family relationships is the attempt to use certain concepts about the family drawn from the social sciences. Why and how this change has occurred in the last decade is a subject for historians. It would appear to be part of a general effort, which began about ten years ago, to develop an interdisciplinary approach to many problems. This effort was itself, I believe, a reaction against the extreme specialization and the intellectual splits that separated both theorists and their related practices. Psychiatrists and anthropologists were among the first to attempt an integration of the basic knowledge of their two disciplines—knowledge about individuals and about mankind. This move towards integration has been followed by many other attempts to build closer relationships between specialists from different social

[1] M. Robert Gomberg, 'Principles and Practices in Counseling', *Diagnosis and Process in Family Counseling*, M. Robert Gomberg and Frances T. Levinson (eds.), Family Service Association of America, 1951, p. 22.

science disciplines and to incorporate the contributions of the basic
sciences into various aspects of social work practice. Such theoretical
knowledge provides, presumably, a foundation upon which the science
of a practice can be built.[1]

The high hopes held in the early days by those who believed that
integration would lead to wider and deeper understanding of how
best to meet human needs have often been frustrated. It is now more
clearly recognized that integration is indeed difficult to effect. In spite
of the difficulties the attempts continue and, I believe, will continue
in the future, although it is generally acknowledged that difficult
intellectual effort will be required and that increasingly effective
practice will come about slowly.

Social work's attempts to draw upon the findings of the social
sciences as well as upon psychiatric knowledge have taken various
forms and have affected both practice and professional education.[2]
This discussion is concerned only with the attempts that have affected
family casework. To realize how widespread is the influence of the
social sciences, one has only to sample the current professional
literature. In some instances, when a foundation has provided funds
for a social scientist to do a piece of experimental work closely related
to practice, the experience has been fully documented. Otto Pollak's
work at the Child Guidance Institute of the Jewish Board of Guardians
is probably the best-known experiment of this kind.[3] However, the
impact of the efforts to use social science concepts in relation to the
family seems to have been felt far beyond the few experimental
projects. The result is apparent in the addition to casework theory
of concepts related specifically to the family as it is studied and
described by the behavioural scientists.

Perhaps the most significant of the social science concepts that has
found a place in social work thinking is the concept of social role.
This concept has been a natural bridge between social work and social
science, since it deals with the linkage between the individual and his
society, and it makes possible an integrated understanding of the
intrapsychic and the social components of behaviour. Many more such
concepts, however, are now familiar to social workers. These include
the concepts of the nuclear family, the family of orientation, the family
of procreation, the socialization of the child, social interaction, and

---

[1] Grace Longwell Coyle, *Social Science in the Professional Education of Social Workers*,
Council on Social Work Education, New York, 1958.
[2] Ibid.
[3] Otto Pollak, *Integrating Sociological and Psychoanalytic Concepts*, Russell Sage
Foundation, New York, 1956.

the effects of sub cultures—ethnic, socio-economic, and geographical—
on the structure, functions, and processes of the families embedded
in them.

As I read the material in which such concepts are discussed, I was
faced with two difficulties. First, I did not know how widespread the
influence of these concepts is. I wondered how familiar they have now
become to the majority of knowledgeable caseworkers interested in
working with the family as a group. Certainly there is no doubt that
the concepts are widely used by those who do the writing. Second,
and more important, I had no way of discovering to what extent an
understanding of such concepts actually affects professional practice.
Do family caseworkers who are equipped with both the concepts of
dynamic psychiatry and the now familiar concepts drawn from the
behavioural sciences conduct themselves differently in dealing with
client families? The use of the latter concepts should enable the caseworker to acquire a more specific, more accurate, and more dynamic
understanding of the environment in which the individual is functioning. Whether this is actually happening, only practising caseworkers
themselves can reveal.

The third movement is the one with which this article is particularly
concerned. It is the suggestion, recurring throughout recent casework
literature, that if caseworkers are going to deal with the family as a
group, they will find a knowledge of small group theory helpful.
Research into small group behaviour and dynamics is one of the most
extensive and most rapidly expanding social science fields. Such study
and research lie within the provinces of both social psychology and
sociology. I have been very much interested to note that the writers
who have made the suggestion that small group theory can be of use
to caseworkers seem to be saying, 'Perhaps the small group theorists
have something to offer.' I have not yet seen any evidence that caseworkers have found useful answers to their concerns or have seized
upon what answers they have with satisfaction.

Hesitancy about using small group theory may well be derived
from a variety of circumstances. One circumstance is the present state
of research in small group theory. Although a great deal of thought
and effort is being put into such studies and into the theories developed
from them,[1] several differing schools of thought are evident. There is
a tendency towards fragmentation. One student or another concentrates
on some single aspect of group behaviour, and relatively few attempts

[1] A. Paul Hare, Edgar F. Borgatta, and Robert Bales (eds.), *Small Groups: Studies in
Social Interaction*, Alfred A. Knopf, New York, 1955.

are made to create a synthesis that will provide a consistent and inclusive system of concepts which will adequately cover the field.

Moreover, from the viewpoint of the caseworker, much of the content of small group theory seems to lack the familiar concept of the individual, which the caseworker is accustomed to use in his thinking. In some instances this omission is due to the use of a different psychological theory, and in some to a complete lack of psychological theory. There is increasing realization among small group theorists of the need to create an integrated approach that utilizes both psychological and sociological concepts, but achievement of this integration is difficult and has not yet been accomplished effectively.

In spite of these difficulties there is considerable evidence of a search for concepts that will be useful in perceiving the family as a group. Professional practice cannot wait until there is a perfect theory available to be applied. A field of practice makes a stab at creating a theory if none exists, or it experiments with whatever imperfect but developing theory is available to see if it will be useful. Such experimentation is evident in several articles in which the writers have either borrowed parts of recognized small group theory, or have brought together several sets of concepts in the search for a more comprehensive approach.

The new element in this approach is the realization that a group is itself a reality that has to be seen and understood as such. This by no means implies some mystic entity floating in the air above the group members. A group can perhaps best be described by the word 'system' —a set of interacting relationships which has a life history of its own, a relation to the larger social and physical environment, a differentiation within its interacting parts, and a constant interaction with individuals as personalities. If this social reality can be recognized and perceived, the first step has been taken towards working with the family as a group. There is considerable evidence that it was this perception that first led caseworkers to turn towards small group theory as a possible source of further clarification of the dynamics of family interaction. It was also this perception which, when group work was born about thirty years ago, led some group workers to embark on the same search—the search for a set of concepts by which to perceive the social reality with which they are dealing.

Group workers have been only partially successful in this endeavour. They are not in agreement on the theoretical base. Such a base does exist in rudimentary and developing form, however, and it is this theoretical base of related concepts which I should like to present here. I am not sure that all of these concepts apply to the family or that their use by caseworkers would meet the apparent need to understand the family as a group. Nevertheless, I think that they furnish a useful base for discussion, and for experimentation and research by a few daring souls.

The framework of generic concepts that is offered here has been developed for the educational purpose of assisting group work students to sharpen their perception of the groups with which they deal and thereby to enhance their ability to make an accurate diagnosis of the group as such and to fulfil their function as professional group workers. It is drawn from small group theory on a somewhat eclectic basis and has been tested and refined as a teaching tool. It has proved to be useful in sharpening workers' perceptions by offering a definition of certain concepts and showing their inter-relationships. Doubtlessly it will be improved as time goes on and will be used increasingly by practitioners as a means of improving the performance of their skills.

The framework presented below deals with six aspects, or dimensions, of the social process within the group. As is true in any analytical approach, the reality is torn apart for the purpose of focusing perception on one or another aspect. It should be clear, however, that the processes described are in constant interaction with each other and occur simultaneously. They change as the group lives. They are affected by its past; they express its present; and, in part, they determine its future. Each of the six aspects of social process within the group will be presented very briefly and with only slight elaboration. Some indication of the use made of it in casework practice will be given.

1. *The Process of Group Formation or Establishment of Group Identity.* What is the process by which a group is born? Given a social setting and a collection of individuals, what accounts for the coagulation of these individuals into a group as a separate entity? What precipitates this coagulation, and what is the process by which it takes place?

Three factors, in combination, determine the initial stages of a group's life and, to some extent, its continuing process: (1) the determination of group goals; (2) the determination of group membership; and (3) the initial type of structure. Obviously these three processes interact. It is only when all three can be discerned that coagulation has taken place and that the group has defined itself as a collectivity within its social environment.

Group goals may or may not be established initially. In some cases a group begins with a number of persons who first get together and then define their goals. This process can be seen in two individuals who become emotionally attached to each other and later take on the goals of marriage and the establishment of a family. In other cases goals are established first, as with individuals who wish to get married in order to establish a family but for whom mates are selected by others—as often happens in other cultures and sometimes happens in our own.

The goals individuals have in becoming members of groups fall into three categories: (1) overt, conscious goals, that is, what the members say about why they belong to a group; (2) implicit but unavowed goals, such as the need for status, recognition, or approval; and (3) unconscious goals. The goals of the group ultimately emerge out of these three types of goals of the individual members. Each group adopts methods by which its goals are defined and are changed as its needs, membership, and purpose change.

According to some authorities the major goal, or purpose, of the family is the socialization of the child. Other acknowledged goals of the family are the preservation of the marital relationship, the maintenance of the family as a unit, and the meeting of individual emotional needs of family members. The significance of one or more of these goals to a particular family will depend on a number of idiosyncratic factors.

The determination of a group's membership, the second factor in group formation, includes such factors as the field from which potential members may be selected (as affected by the goals of the group and by the nature of its social environment), the size of the group, and the changing character of the group relationships over a period of time.

In the formation of the family, the selective process is first set in operation around the choice of a mate. Personal, cultural, and other social factors limit and define the areas from which this selection may take place. The nuclear family, composed of husband, wife, and children, is the smallest, most exclusive, and most intimate group in our society. Family size is increased by lateral extension (aunts, uncles, and cousins—relatives of the present generation) and by vertical extension (grandparents). The nuclear family may incorporate any or all of these extensions within its group, but the prevailing American urban pattern is for the nuclear family to be isolated from the extended family, at least insofar as residence is concerned.

The third factor in group formation is the initial type of group structure. The chief function of structure is to further the evolvement of expected ways of proceeding and of relating, so that the group can achieve its goals. In the family the implicit and explicit rules, and the clarification of roles, that lead members to know what to expect from each other develop out of the structure. The relationship of the family's goals to its effective functioning has been studied and commented upon in terms of 'goal-directedness'. It has been shown that the healthy family is the one that is able to pursue goals for the good of the whole, while the 'sick' family has difficulty in planning anything for the family members to do as a group.

Group structure is influenced by its relation to time and space. In the dimension of time, two factors assume importance. One is that the family must be geared to continuity in time. The other is that the family must be able to change its structure to accommodate the changes within the family itself which affect the role expectations, purposes, and functioning of family members. As the children grow from infancy through childhood and adolescence into young adulthood, and as they finally separate from the nuclear family, the family structure must be able to change to meet the changing needs, capacities, and purposes. The family is rooted in the past through its heritage and its traditions, but it also looks to the future, to the continuation of the family in coming generations.

The influence of space on family structure refers to the place in which the nuclear family is united, the home. The home is the chief arena of family interaction. As such, it takes on symbolic meaning for family members. The physical aspects of the home—the comfort and beauty it provides, the space available in which things can be done collectively and individually, the adequacy of the home in comparison with other homes in the family's social environment—have a bearing on the family members' performance and fulfillment of role expectations.

2. *Interpersonal Relations or Interaction*. This dimension of social process, the relations operating between individuals in a group, has three aspects: (1) the status, or ranking, process; (2) sub groups; and (3) role structure. The status, or ranking, process is a process of evaluation by which each individual is assigned a particular place on a collective scale. Various factors influence the ranking process: the values that determine each position, the intensity of the members' competitiveness for particular positions, the simplicity or complexity of the value scales used by the group, the relation of the rating to the group's goals, the impact on the ranking process of the values of the

surrounding society and culture, and the creation of either high status members or stigmatized members.

In relation to the family group, one can say that the father's status within the family is affected by the position he holds in the larger community—including his job, the nature of his social contacts, and his fulfilment of the role expectations of father and husband, Each child may be assessed according to his academic achievement, popularity, conformity, appearance, and sex-adequate behaviour (masculinity and femininity). The values that determine the ranking process may be influenced by personality as well as by social factors.

Every group has sub groups within it which reflect the personal choices and the likes and dislikes of group members. The family group has been described as a system with three sub systems: the marital relationship, the parent-child relationship, and the sibling relationship.[1] Within each of these sub systems there are intensities of relationship which may affect the relationships of any other sub system or of the group as a whole. The intensity of a child's relationship with a particular parent may be related to role and division of responsibility. The mother-infant relationship is by its very nature one of intense feeling. The mother may continue to play the major role in the rearing of the young child as part of the family plan to keep the mother-child relationship strong. As a rule, this continued close relationship does not interfere with the development of a significant father-child relationship, although at times the mother-child relationship is prolonged on an intensive level beyond the child's need for it. Sometimes a parent and a child develop particular attachments that tend to exclude other family members from the relationship—the mother and son against the father and daughter, for example. These attachments may damage relationships in the total group and in each sub-system—the parents, the parents and children, and the siblings.

The role structure of the family has to do with the definition of what is to be done and who is to do it. The roles of family members are influenced by the family's particular ethnic or class affiliation.

3. *Group Control and the Exercise of Authority.* The authority structure, the structure developed to create and distribute power, is in part related to the group's goals, but it has characteristics that cannot be described in those terms alone. Uniting efforts of several individuals to achieve common or similar ends requires that each one exert control over part of himself in his relations with the others.

[1] Otto Pollak and Donald Brieland, 'The Mid-west Seminar on Family Diagnosis and Treatment', *Social Casework*, Vol. XLII, No. 7 (1961), pp. 319-24.

Authority, the power to enforce such controls, is established either by common consent or by the autocratic rules of the strongest. The psychological aspects of authority for both the wielder of authority and the governed deserve consideration.

The source of authority in the family is implied in the terms 'matriarchal family' and 'patriarchal family'. Recently the term 'democratic family' has come into usage. This term implies authority shared by the parents, who gradually involve their children in the control of family affairs by allowing them to learn to make decisions during the transition between childhood and adulthood. Authority is also exercised within the family's various sub groups.

4. *Group Thinking as a Basis for Action as a Group.* This aspect of group process has to do with the process of communication between members and with decision making. Communication is both verbal and non-verbal. Meaning is conveyed by connotation as well as by denotation. Tone of voice and bodily responses (facial expressions in particular) often communicate more than words; sometimes they underscore the words spoken and sometimes they even contradict them. In a family that is functioning well, each member usually preceives the intent of the words and other signs of communication of other family members and responds appropriately. Family agencies are well aware that there are situations in which family communication breaks down and barriers are erected that make subsequent communicative efforts more difficult. Such disruptions may be caused by problems in interpersonal relations, by internal problems of one of the family members, or by inability to state clearly what is meant.

Decision making should be looked at in relation to group structure. In assessing the process of decision making in the family, one must understand the family's usual ways of functioning and determine who is involved in making decisions and wielding authority. Basic steps that must be followed in decision making are (1) becoming aware of the problem; (2) clarifying and evaluating proposed solutions; (3) reaching a decision; and (4) acting upon the decision that has been reached.

Conflict is a component of every family's interacting experiences. The manner in which the family handles and resolves conflict is one primary criterion of its relative stability. As family members face a problem and work together to find a solution, the family group itself is strengthened.

5. *Emotional Aspects of Group Behaviour.* The emotional aspects of group behaviour are the most difficult aspects to assess. They are

primarily concerned with group cohesiveness and group morale. Cohesiveness is the degree of attachment members feel towards the group as a whole. Morale is the feeling of the members about the group as expressed in the level of their motivation to attack group tasks.

6. *The Value System or Group Culture.* The value system is the pattern of values that evolves out of the group's life. It determines the norms of behaviour for group members and for the group as a whole. Such values may include (1) beliefs concerning right and wrong, and ideas or ideologies; (2) appreciative or aesthetic values related to what is considered appropriate or beautiful; and (3) cultural values.

Each person has a system of values as part of his heritage, values he has taken on largely from his own family, from prestige figures, and from his social environment. When two persons form a group through marriage, they will inevitably influence each other. As a result, a new modified set of values to which both agree will evolve. In the socialization of children, values are inculcated in the children chiefly by the parents. As the children are exposed to influences outside the family, they will derive other values that will in turn influence the value pattern of the family group.

I should like to comment on the use that can be made of such a framework and some of the difficulties it presents. My attempt to develop a framework of concepts for use by students and practitioners has rested on a firm belief that without suitable concepts, perception is random, fragmented, and often blind. As one writer has said, '*What we perceive, or overlook, in the field of our potential experience depends on the framework of concepts we have in our minds.*'—Moreover, these concepts with which we approach psychological and social reality are distorted by certain emotional (individually conditioned) and ideological (collectively conditioned) factors. We are thus prevented from making significant observations and from asking relevant questions. The 'obvious' facts are indeed obvious; still they cannot be grasped until we possess adequate descriptive concepts enabling us to perform these tasks.[1]

To prove that this is so, one has only to cite the illumination of the understanding of the individual which followed the acceptance by the casework field of the concepts of dynamic psychiatry.

Pollak has pointed out that when a term, such as 'psychosocial', offers the thinker two differing levels of perception, the result is likely

[1] Gustav Ichheiser, 'Misunderstandings in Human Relations', *American Journal o, Sociology*, Vol. 55, No. 2 (1949), Part 2, p. 2.

to be biased or incomplete thinking.[1] At present, in most social work thinking, the 'psycho' part of this term is understood on the basis of a specific theory about personality, but the 'social' part of the term is perceived in very general and often vague terms. The environment, or background, is perceived only dimly, at very high levels of generalization, while the individual in all his dynamic psychological reality is retained in the foreground. The acceptance and use of such sociological terms as 'nuclear family' or 'socio-cultural patterns' have served to make the background somewhat more concrete, and therefore have heightened the social worker's perception of the true place of background in the psychosocial situation. When one attempts, however, to understand the family as a group, or the individual within the family, one must have as concrete, as well founded, and as fully perceived concepts about the family as about the individual. It is for this reason that the struggle to create such a framework of generic concepts is worth the effort.

One of the traps into which one is likely to fall is the too ready adoption of a framework that is familiar and therefore seems to solve a problem easily. In terms of our present considerations, this leads to two common and dangerous practices that illustrate the fallacy of argument by analogy. The first is personification of the group and then the application to it of the familiar and comforting concepts that have so successfully illuminated our understanding of the individual. Such fallacious reasoning usually appears in the form of discussions of the 'collective ego', the 'group personality', or even the 'group mind'. The writer then moves easily from that assumption to a discussion of a 'group neurosis' or a 'group psychosis'. Occasionally sympathetic caseworkers who have listened to my exposition of the group have exclaimed, 'Now I see! You are talking about the group id and the group superego.' Psychiatrists and caseworkers have a tendency to adopt an anthropomorphic approach to the group. The tendency is equally dangerous, however, for both professions. When an analogy is used as a basis for action, it may well deceive us as to the real nature of the reality. However much we may wish it, a group is not, and never becomes, a personality. A group is a system produced by personalities in interaction with each other and with the group's surrounding society. To describe and perceive the group accurately, one needs to use the tools of thought appropriate to its reality, that is, the concepts that deal with collective behaviour and social interaction.

[1] Otto Pollak, op. cit.

A second type of argument by analogy appears in the literature of both social workers and social scientists. This consists of utilizing concepts developed in other scientific areas—often those that have high prestige in the general culture. This kind of cultural borrowing is perhaps inevitable, but I believe that an informed and sophisticated thinker needs to be aware that here too he may distort the reality. Homeostasis, field of forces, balance, equilibrium, vector, and valence —terms drawn from various scientific disciplines—are appearing with increased frequency in the theoretical formulations of social work.

Many years ago Eduard Lindeman pointed out in a very valuable little book, *Social Discovery*, the place and the danger of argument by analogy. 'Analogy is frequently used as a substitute for logic . . . The social sciences, if they are to be in fact sciences, must evolve a method which goes beyond analogy.'[1] It is inevitable, of course, that use will be made of familiar patterns of thought. There is a place for the poetry of analogy as well as the prose of careful definition. As we attempt, however, to increase our understanding of the family as a group let us not fall into this easy trap of using analogies that comfort us by their familiarity or their status but that may, in the end, confuse our perception and our actions.

To make use of a theoretical formulation in practice, one must do more than listen to a lecture or two, or read a few books. One must become immersed in the content of the theory and in its implications, and must constantly assess its relevance to the particular practice in which one is engaged.

[1] Eduard C. Lindeman, *Social Discovery*, Republic Publishing Co., New York, 1924, pp. 50-51.

3

THE NATURE OF MARITAL INTERACTION*

LILY PINCUS

IN talking about the nature of marital interaction we do this from our experience with the marriage problems of those couples who come for help to the Family Discussion Bureau. This Bureau is a social casework unit within the aegis of the Tavistock Institute for Human Relations, working in close co-operation with psychiatric consultants from the Tavistock Clinic. In addition to a casework service for marriages in trouble, the Bureau offers training to other professional caseworkers who have to deal either with overt marriage problems or with the manifestations of marital tensions presented to them in other symptoms.

This paper, like all the Bureau's publications, is the product of the staff group's collaborative effort. We can therefore draw not only on the experience of our own casework, but also upon material which we have gathered in our training groups. These have provided convincing evidence that at whatever agency people ask for help, and whatever problems they present, the processes of marital interaction which are exposed once a certain depth of understanding has been reached, show fundamentally the same elements. So far, we have only been able to study these processes in unhappy or unsatisfactory marriages in which the partners turn, or are directed, to professional sources for help. I want, therefore, to illustrate the theme of this paper by talking about overt marriage problems and the way we see them at the Family Discussion Bureau.

There is no marriage without conflict, and at times, in all marriages, the predominance of loving feelings is threatened by the frustrations

* Published in *The Marital Relationship as a Focus for Casework*, The Codicote Press, London, 1962.

and anxieties which inevitably arise. Those who seek help at such a point may have particular difficulties in tolerating emotional conflict, but seeking help also indicates some hope and some degree of willingness to go on with the relationship. Even though clients may insist that their marriage is hopeless and that they must separate, coming to a place like the Family Discussion Bureau can be taken as investment in the agency of their often unrecognized hopes of staying together. They hand these over to the caseworker who is seen as someone whose job it is to prevent marriage breakdown. While this is, of course, fundamentally the function of the Bureau, the caseworker needs to be aware of the ambivalence in the client when the latter thrusts such demands upon him. Similarly, a couple demanding help with separation at a probation office may have the unrecognized hope that their impulse to break up the home will be controlled. In the face of explosive and distressing emotional conflict, one or both partners may fear that the bad feelings which have arisen in the marriage are too dangerous and cannot be contained. They may then feel that it is possible to escape danger by breaking up the marriage. In such a crisis couples are not infrequently advised by friends, and sometimes even by professional workers, to separate. Unless the situation has been fully explored, the limitation and ineffectiveness of 'advice' are self-evident. Whether given explicitly, or implicitly through an anxious response to the situation, advice to separate often represents a collusion with the fantasies of one partner or the other. It may be saying in effect: 'You need not change: there is someone who will love you as you are.' Understanding and acceptance of the client's ambivalent feelings may, however, help him to accept his inner conflicts about love and hate, and to come to terms with them sufficiently to make his own choice. This is not to argue that all marriages can be made wholly satisfying relationships; but we have come to believe that there are potentialities for growth in most, and that work focused on the marriage affords a 'good therapeutic wicket'.

The experience of social workers and doctors has shown that over the last ten years, more and more people have asked for help with their marriage problems, and have thus expressed a sense of hope that help can be given.

The changed attitude towards seeking help springs partly from the gradual assimilation within the community of knowledge about the nature and importance of intimate family relationships. Psychoanalytic concepts about personality development and personal relationships have infiltrated into many areas of contemporary life; in particular there is widespread recognition of the fundamental influence of the child's early relationships on his later attitudes to others. This concept is for us the key to marital work since we see marriage as the direct heir of childhood relationships. Where these have been predominantly negative, in reality or fantasy, or too laden with anxiety, negative and destructive forces may become predominant in the relationship between husband and wife. The girl who always rebelled against a violent father or mother, may marry a man by whom she feels persecuted and with whom she seems to repeat something of the experiences she had with the parents; the man who felt resentful towards a dominant mother may choose a wife who makes him feel equally powerless and dependent.

Although there is often a wish to start afresh in marriage and to escape the frustrations or disappointments of unsatisfactory early relationships, the strong unconscious ties to the first love-objects may help to determine the choice of a partner with whom the earlier situation can be compulsively re-enacted. Marriages which find their way to helping agencies are mostly those in which these negative elements present great obstacles to change and growth. The unconscious residues in the personality of earlier conflicts, fantasies which are charged with anxiety or guilt, may 'match up' so that each partner reacts to the other in ways which perpetuate rather than resolve the conflicts and intensify the fantasies which they dare not risk putting to the test of reality. Thus, the partners may be held in a pattern of mutual inhibition, or in a mutually punishing and self-depriving interaction, or a pattern of dependence, or dominance, which confirms their secret fears about their worthlessness, or destructiveness. An understanding of how such conflicts and fantasies have arisen out of the experiences of earlier life and how they can reduce capacity to build up mutually satisfying relationships in adulthood throws light on the apparently irrational behaviour of husbands and wives. It is the unconscious elements which account for the intractable nature of marital discord, often in spite of the partners' desperate wish, at a conscious level, to behave differently.

Where a precarious balance between love and hate has been achieved in the marriage, the positive forces in it may be strengthened, or threatened, as new situations arise. Circumstances which for one couple evoke a positive response and a strengthening of the relationship constitute a threat to another. In general, a degree of negative 'fit' between the partners implies limitation in the flexibility of the relationship and in the partners' capacity to adjust to changed circumstances or disturbing events. A marital crisis which appears to have been caused by financial stress, housing difficulty, the birth of a baby, the illness or death of a parent, has therefore to be understood not only as an isolated event. The couple's response to the impact of such external occurrence is an expression of some aspect of their relationship. Each partner will cope with an event in accordance with the meaning it has in his own inner world and in the emotional equilibrium between both of them.

The response of husband and wife to a first baby, for instance, will depend very largely on their own experiences, at unconscious levels in relation to father and mother and siblings. The husband who is seeking in his wife an ideal, all-loving, never-rejecting mother will find it difficult to tolerate a 'rival'. His very need for an exclusive relationship may have motivated his choice of a girl who herself has difficulties in sharing, perhaps because of difficulties in sharing father with mother. When a baby arrives, she may withdraw from her husband, thus intensifying his difficulties. This is one of many familiar patterns of interaction which may create strain when the change from a two-person to a three-person relationship constitutes a new situation in the marriage. The reversal to a two-person situation when the children are leaving the home, may be equally critical. I am thinking of a couple where the wife threatened to leave her husband after the marriage of their only daughter. Both partners had used the daughter as a container for all their loving feelings, and also as a wall, a protection against their destructive feelings for each other—and were terrified about what would happen if this wall was removed. The casework process helped to show them that the wall had also stopped them from making contact with each other, seeing each other as real people, and becoming aware of their need for, and dependence on, each other. This couple had married against the wishes of both sets of parents and felt that their marriage had never been sanctioned.

Trouble of the kind and degree which moves or forces people to seek help with marriages is a sign that something is wrong with the personalities involved—a symptom like many others. For those concerned with marital work, it raises the question: 'What does this symptom mean for the marriage as a whole; how does it affect the total economy of the family?' This question implies the basic conception that each marriage is an entity with its own characteristic pattern which is not only the sum total of the personalities of the two partners, but the product of the processes of interaction between them.

It is now generally accepted that in work of a psychotherapeutic nature, and that includes certain kinds of casework, there is a need to relate to the 'whole person', the 'total personality'. This means responding to the 'whole person' of a client, including those aspects of his personality of which he is not aware, and in this way finding, and responding, to a more complete person in him than he is aware of being.[1]

In marital work the unrecognized, or unconscious aspect of a client's personality is very often revealed in the partner. This offers the caseworker an opportunity to help husband and wife to recognize in each other those hitherto disowned parts of themselves which often represent the very opposite of those aspects of their personalities which are more acceptable and of which they are aware.

The therapeutic effectiveness of marital work lies in the possibility of helping each partner to recognize, as a step on the difficult road towards accepting and tolerating them, the denied or rejected aspects of himself which they have found in or projected on to their partner. The conflict and confusion between the partners can be seen as an attempt to integrate the contradicting parts, to get them 'married' inside themselves.

A passive, quiet man who hated unpleasantness, married a girl who rowed about everything and with everybody and who was extremely aggressive towards him. She was a tall, angular woman with somewhat masculine features who dressed incongruously in bright colours and wore flowery hats—the only overt expression of her wish to be more feminine. She was a very sick woman who suffered from a congenital heart disease and her frequent violent outbursts naturally aggravated her illness. She drove herself into constant activity, and passionately and viciously fought against her husband's slowness and quietness, the very qualities which she needed in him and in herself. His mother had always been an invalid and, as a boy, he had to give up all his pleasures to look after her and the home. He insisted that he had missed nothing, that he only loved and adored his mother, and he was extremely upset about his wife's unkindness and aggressiveness to her. During casework it became clear that his own resentment and anger with his sick suffering mother had been so incompatible with his love and concern for her that he could not tolerate it in himself. He married a wife who could express it for him, and he unconsciously encouraged her to be the attacker by abdicating his masculine aggres-

[1] Harold F. Searles, 'The Effort to Drive the Other Person Crazy—An Element in the Aetiology and Psychotherapy of Schizophrenia', *British Journal of Medical Psychology*, Vol. XXXII, Part 1, 1959.

sion to her, making her express, as it were, both her own and his. This was the most striking feature of the complex interaction between this couple.

When the husband became less terrified of what he had felt to be his destructive masculinity, he could be more constructively manly; his wife could then relax and calm down and her health improved considerably. There was no great change in the personalities of either husband or wife, but even some small development in the direction of self-integration will help towards health and maturity, both in the individual and in the marriage relationship.

It is not always the 'badness' that is projected on to the partner, sometimes it is the 'goodness'. One partner may see him or herself as worthless and inferior, and keep the other on a pedestal to be worshipped and admired. This, too, may be an unconscious attempt to cope with hate and destructive feelings. One husband, who insisted on keeping his wife on a pedestal, said, in the course of his treatment: 'If I think of her in any other way, I'm afraid she'll fall down, pedestal and all, and be buried under the debris.'

There can be no meaningful relationship without interaction, both of a positive and of a negative kind; processes of projection and identification go on in all relationships and can be either creative, or inhibiting or frustrating. In marriage, an intense emotional relationship between two adults of more or less equal maturity, one involving all areas of life, the pattern of interaction can be seen most clearly and are revealed and highlighted in the choice of partner.

In satisfactory marriages this interaction is essentially benevolent and gratifying to both. Disturbed marriages are those where, on balance, the interaction has become preponderantly negative. This implies that marriage problems are hardly ever 'caused' primarily by one partner or the other. They are almost always the result of a collusion, an unconscious agreement between the couple, probably the same collusion, the same sense of 'fit', which originally brought them together.

Mr X., for example, is a correct somewhat dull husband whose main interest is in facts and figures. He married a lively exciting imaginative girl, and needs her vitality and stimulation. His wife chose him because she needs his control, his 'down-to-earthness'. Both, consciously or unconsciously, agreed to supply what the other one needed. Yet later, the husband finds her intolerable and complains about her incompetence in practical things, while the wife finds him frustrating and boring. Both are no longer aware of the positive potentialities which were inherent in their choice, potentialities which are still present in the marriage.

In this instance the positive feelings had remained accessible, but there are, of course, also cases in which the love and the drive towards maturity and integration have become so overlaid with hate and destructive feelings that casework cannot reach them. A vital factor in determining the accessibility of positive forces in the marriage lies in the caseworker's attitudes, her awareness of the processes of interaction. She cannot gain access until she knows in what direction to try.

Working with the marriage relationship does not, therefore, simply mean seeing both partners, or trying reconciliation. It does not mean accepting the complaints of the one who appears to be the victim, or trying to 'change' the other. Paradoxically, it means just the opposite; looking at the individual who comes and trying to understand what he or she is doing in this marriage, what is being unconsciously expressed for him by the other, what of his own internal conflicts he is unconsciously trying to solve in what is going on. If there is strife, it may well be that the strife is the client's internal conflict externalized and acted out in this way. In other words, we have always to be looking for the unseen and unexpressed aspects of the client's personality which he will be showing to us in his picture of his partner and will reveal in his relationship with the caseworker.

It has been said that an optimist is someone who has a depressed friend. This is not just a joke when we are talking of marriages and of families. The person who complains of his partner's depression, dependence, or dominance may well, by denying his own, leave the partner to express a double dose and, at the same time, by developing defensive opposite attitudes to the denied ones, increase the stress and the estrangement in the marriage.

Mr Carter had been suffering since his adolescence from bouts of depression. He is now in his early forties, has been married for sixteen years and has three teenage children. Recently, he had been so depressed that he insisted on being admitted to a mental hospital. After six weeks' in-patient treatment he was referred to the Family Discussion Bureau as his psychiatrist felt that his patient's illness reflected some strain in his marriage.

In his interview at the Bureau it emerged that the recent depression had closely followed his promotion to the job he had wanted for many years—and he constantly brought material which showed how terrifying it was to him to be a success. He told his caseworker that his father had worked far beyond his physical resources to enable his only child to go to grammar school. When the boy was eighteen, his father died and it was then that Mr Carter had his first breakdown. During casework it became clear that this sequence of events was an expression of his unconscious conviction that for him, any real success in life could only be at the expense of others. This theme was brought up at every interview and elaborated by other stories, e.g. he only got his present job when the personnel manager, who had turned down his repeated earlier applications, had a heart-attack and was forced to retire. This had confirmed his fears—that he could be successful only at the expense of others. One way out was to be a failure, helpless and sick. At home he was always tired and depressed, spending most week-ends in bed, withdrawing from his family whom he felt to be unsympathetic to his suffering. He seemed unable to let his wife see the successful well-functioning aspects of his personality, yet he constantly complained that she was 'belittling' him.

Mrs Carter, a big, cheerful, competent woman, who had never known a day's illness, coped well with the home and the children. She felt that she had to keep the family going, that everything depended on her. As only the minimum of her husband's very good salary came into the household (the rest just vanished, he didn't seem to know how!) she too had a full-time job. Although often angry with her husband, she had come to accept him as another rather tiresome child, from whom she could expect neither help nor support—and treated him accordingly.

The same rigid role-distribution which governed the relationship between this couple had developed between their son and one daughter, the successful girl being the replica of her mother, the awkward stammering boy being seen by both parents as a problem child who, one day, would be exactly like his father. The boy attended a child guidance clinic. When we discussed the case with his therapist, it became clear how much the success of the boy's treatment depended on an understanding of what went on between his parents.

When Mr Carter first came to the Bureau he said that the hospital stay, while helping him not to be completely overwhelmed by his depression, had really made life more difficult. He had always seen himself as an individual patient, but now he had been given to understand that there was something in the relationship with his wife which reactivated his ambivalent feelings for his mother who had been very possessive of him. Apparently, he said, he had married the wrong woman, somebody who made his illness worse and he could not see what the Bureau could do to help. For some time he began each session by expressing these doubts and he showed his strong drive to remain an individual patient. Although he complained about his wife's lack of sympathy and understanding, he did not really want to make an effort which might effect a change in the marriage relationship.

Mrs Carter was at first very resentful that, through her husband, she was 'dragged' into treatment which she certainly did not need and she was angry with her caseworker who, she felt, was blaming her for her husband's illness. Soon, however, she began to see how she had always to deny any weakness, need and dependence in herself, and what a tremendous strain this had been. Even as a child she had always to be bright and cheerful. Her parents disapproved of 'moods'; and anyhow they had enough worries with her brother, a brilliant boy, who suddenly at the age of twelve developed a mysterious and frightening illness.

In the couse of treatment, Mrs Carter became more vulnerable and depressed; more doubtful about herself, wondering how her attitude might affect others, her husband, her children, and how much she might have contributed to her husband's and her son's difficulties.

The panic of clients at the first indication of change is a common experience to all caseworkers and therapists. It affects them as well as the people they are trying to help, who now make them feel that 'things are getting worse'. The panic arises from the threat to the previous equilibrium, which, though unhappy and painful, was at least familiar and represented the best compromise then available to them. Any threat to this situation raises great anxieties about what is going to happen now. If both husband and wife are in treatment, both can simultaneously work through the changes in themselves and the partner, as well as their resistance against them and the resultant 'unknown'. I hope to show later in this paper how the Carters were helped to understand, and thus to modify, their denial and mutual projections.

Projections of disowned, repressed wishes, needs and drives onto the partner, and the mutually destructive processes which this may entail, can be seen as the underlying dynamic in a great many marital problems. The hardworking wife, who keeps herself, her home and her children meticulously clean and runs from agency to agency to complain about her dirty drunkard of a husband, may well be worried about the bad, dirty aspects of herself, perhaps her 'bad' sexuality. It may be this anxiety about herself which makes it so important for her

D

to keep all the 'bad' things firmly fixed onto the husband. Her demands for help may express, on one level, her need for reassurance that she is good and he is bad, and on another level an unconscious striving to relieve herself of her guilt about herself which has been intolerably increased by her destructiveness towards her husband.

The rigid man with high moral standards who is desperately anxious about his slovenly, promiscuous, or delinquent wife, may need her to express similar drives of his own which he has never dared to face and has repressed into the unconscious. The husband or wife who is determined that the other one is 'mad' and must be 'put away', may well be fighting off his or her own madness. How often have we to ask ourselves: 'Who is the patient?' In trying to help such couples we must remember that one partner is never simply the victim of the other. His personality almost certainly contains elements which offer some reality basis for projection. The unconscious 'arrangement' between the spouses must also offer some sort of satisfaction to both. They may, therefore, not be easily prepared to give it up, however painful it may be, as we have just seen in the case of the Carters.

In work with a heterosexual relationship of intense emotional involvement, such processes of projection often express anxiety about masculinity or femininity, and confusion about sexual roles—an underlying factor in most marriage problems. Each partner's doubts about playing his own role effectively may make him feel that the other is trying to force him or her into a rigid pattern. 'If only she (or he) stopped nagging, I would be all right.' The husband who is worried about his adequacy as a man, the wife who has doubts about herself as a proper woman, will feel, 'If only I had a different partner (a more feminine wife, a more masculine husband) all would be well.'

Yet both the wish for a more 'manly' or 'womanly' partner, and the conviction that this would make everything 'all right' and enable them to become more masculine or more feminine themselves, are likely to be an illusion. Neither has, in fact, chosen a partner who more closely represents the ideal of masculinity or femininity, although they have probably met such people. Each may need unconsciously to avoid a situation in which he might be confronted with, and have to respond to, the proper masculinity or femininity of his fantasy. This fantasy also has unwelcome or even terrifying aspects which he therefore fears, both in himself and in his partner. When such couples come to a helping agency their overt request is likely to be for change;

change of themselves and the partner. Yet their most urgent need may be for help to tolerate themselves with their conflicts and contradictions. This will permit greater tolerance towards the partner and result in a lessening of anxiety which may then make it possible for both to play their appropriate roles more effectively.

We have spoken so much about processes of projection because it is these which can perhaps most easily be observed. But there are many other mechanisms which may come into play as patterns of relationship develop between husband and wife.

Obviously, not everyone will choose an 'opposite' type of partner. Many people need to strengthen the image they have of themselves by marrying someone with whom they can closely identify. Such couples often present a picture of good companionship, of seeing eye to eye and never having rows. Here it is difference which is feared, and an important function of such a collusion may be to maintain a denial of their sexual difference and thus to avoid the envy, or anxiety, or aggressive feelings which might be aroused by the realization of it. If this is the case, the apparent harmony can only be preserved at a cost and it is generally the strain felt in attempting a sexual relationship, which must at the same time be severely restricted, which brings such couples to the Bureau. 'We could be so happy if it weren't for sex; we have so much in common', they may say, or, 'If only we could just live like brother and sister'. As we work with them it becomes clear how the shared denial of negative feelings, and their need to keep differences, rivalries and disagreement out of the marriage, is restricting self-expression and frustrating the natural drives to mature and to develop their adult sexual roles.

The need to identify, and the task of differentiation, are central in every marriage. But there are people who cannot easily exist as individuals and have an intense fear of separateness. They are likely to choose a partner who is equally unsure of himself and the two then cling together like Siamese twins, making further growth and the differentiation of each impossible. These couples may have an apparently satisfactory sexual relationship in which they feel they merge and become 'one'; but they come to the Bureau because of violent rows which seem to arise from their inability to tolerate any wish of one or the other to make an individual move, to have individual possessions, privacy, or feelings, or needs of their own. One woman expressed her predicament when she said, 'You must help us to separate so that we can stay together'. Marriage affords at one and the same time an opportunity for growth and maturation and for a return to and a repetition of the central aspects of past experiences. To most people, for the first time since early childhood, marriage offers the opportunity for an exclusive two-person relationship; for close physical intimacy and the experience of giving and receiving direct bodily satisfaction. It is not a coincidence that lovers sometimes use 'baby talk', or that we refer to 'love-play'. This situation, while offering great potential satisfactions is liable to reactivate what are felt to have been the 'bad' as well as the 'good' experiences of childhood. At both conscious and unconscious levels, husbands and wives transfer on to each other feelings for the important people of the past, and unresolved conflicts from these earlier phases of development are thus likely to be stirred into life again. This makes the marriage relationship especially open to a richness of emotional experience and, by the same token, renders it particularly vulnerable to emotional disturbances. The re-living in marriage of intense childhood feelings can be very frightening to husband and wife. It is therefore particularly important in marital work to be aware of these anxieties, as well as of the part which apparent 'regression' can play in a maturing process.

We have found that emotional disturbances which express themselves in marriage difficulties, and can be seen and dealt with in an adult situation and explored in relation to the processes of interaction between the couple, offer good therapeutic prospects. The very fact that the partners' internal conflicts are externalized in something so central and vital as the marriage relationship, makes them accessible and allows a relatively small change and growth in the individual to pay large dividends in their family life. There are many other factors which make the marriage relationship a particularly effective point of entry for therapeutic intervention: the fundamental drive in most couples to maintain their marriage; the increasing investment in marriage in our urban communities; the support which society gives to marriage as a social institution and, most important of all, the fact that the marriage relationship is, in itself, a dynamic system, in which the most powerful feelings, both 'good' and 'bad', can be expressed and contained. This concept of marriage as a 'container' is of tremendous value in marital work, not only to clients, but perhaps still more to the caseworkers who have to become part of this containing process. This is particularly true for work with very disturbed people who often have a great need for and dependence upon their family relationships, yet are in constant danger of destroying them by their demands and destructiveness. The workers' acceptance of them as marital partners and parents rather than as sick and isolated individuals seems to strengthen their often precarious sense of reality and to provide an opportunity for them to test out the more frightening aspects of the personalities with some measure of safety. The fact that, in marital work, both partners are seen, implies in itself that the rejected and feared aspects of the self, which may have been projected on to the partner, are acceptable and may be controlled and that even destructiveness and 'madness' can somehow be contained in the marriage.

Let us have another look at Mr and Mrs Carter, the couple with the depressed husband and the cheerful managing wife.

Mrs Carter made a warm and dependent relationship with her caseworker. It became very important to her to be understood and accepted, even though she had revealed her 'weakness'. With the caseworker, she felt she could be 'another person'. She recalled with some anxiety that she could also feel this other aspect of herself in the sexual relationship. There she could be passionate and yielding, wanting her husband to be strong and giving. So far she had hardly ever dared to show this for fear that her husband would either use her weakness against her, or that her sexual passion would harm him.

Mr Carter, who was always hiding the successful parts of his personality from his wife and only showed her his weakness, was testing out with his caseworker whether these different aspects of himself could become more integrated and need no longer be so desperately kept apart. She seemed to represent to him the idealized 'good' mother to whom he could trust himself and whom he would not harm, until she told him of her impending holiday. He then revealed, in his interviews, his hatred of the women on whom he feels dependent, his fury at being deserted and also his terror about the impact of these aggressive feelings. Later, he was able to recognize that whenever he had had similar feelings towards his wife, he got ill. For example, his most serious bout of depression had occurred when his wife had taken the children for a holiday abroad to see her brother. This trip had been planned jointly by the couple. Mr Carter agreed to it; he was otherwise engaged and would not have been able to go. But he felt miserable without his wife and the children and thought at the time that it was this that made him ill. Now he became aware that on this, as on other occasions, he got ill when he had been terrified by the strength of his angry feelings which might either harm his family on their journey, or make them hate him so that they would never return. 'I felt the same towards you today,' he said to his case-worker.

That Mr Carter was able to become aware, within the context of the relationship with his caseworker, of the connection between his aggressive feelings towards those on whom he felt dependent, his fear of being successful, and his flight into illness and depression; that Mrs Carter was able to test out with her caseworker whether she could risk showing her weakness and dependence, was a first and funda-mental step towards a redistribution of forces between this couple, and the beginning of more satisfactory and constructive relationships within the whole family. That such insights do not come easily, that they cannot be put to use without struggle and set-backs, goes without saying. The Carters are a current case with the usual ups and downs. But, at present, it seems that the husband's depressive moods have receded and he has become more active and effective in his personal life. His wife, who had to have a minor operation, allowed herself prolonged rest and convalescence. She was surprised how well every-thing went during her absence and can now show her husband how much she needs him. The greatest change can perhaps be seen in the boy, who is happier, more sociable and stammers much less. Having broken down their compulsively maintained and inadequate con-ceptions of each other, we can hope that this family will be able to develop further in their readjusted roles even after casework has been terminated.

I have tried to convey an outline of the processes of marital inter-action as we have come to understand them through our work with overt marriage problems. I have not attempted to show our methods and techniques, in particular the way in which we use our under-standing in our relationship with our clients, as this paper is concerned with the nature of marital interaction rather than with the application of its theory through the medium of a particular technique which can-not be considered without reference to the setting in which it was practised.

Irrespective of setting, a large proportion of problems confronting caseworkers are either overt marriage difficulties or those in which stress in the relationship is displaced on to or is disguised by other symptoms. Once it becomes possible to understand what lies behind the presenting symptoms and the circumstances that give them their outward structure and form, the common elements of family relation-ships emerge and the same aetiology and dynamic principles which determine human growth and behaviour apply. The assumption is that the better these basic human phenomena can be understood, the more effectively will workers in each field be able to develop their own appropriate skills and techniques in the light of the resources available to them in their own settings.

4

TREATMENT IN THE HOME*

RACHEL A. LEVINE

MUCH has been written and said about low-income, multi-problem families and about their apparent resistance to social agency services, especially to mental health clinics. The reasons given run something like this: These are uneducated people who are socially and culturally impoverished, who know hardship, even brutality, who are often teetering on the edge of hunger and despair. They feel alien to middle-class values and are alienated from the rest of society.

Social workers know many of the reasons for these conditions but too little still about ways of combating them so that these people can use the resources the community has to offer in order to improve their lot. Perhaps this is because, despite the sharp contrast in standards and values, social workers nevertheless expect this group to make the big leap from one milieu and its values to another that is wholly unfamiliar, to which they feel hostile, and which is hostile towards them.

'Treatment in the home' is an approach being used in an experimental way by the Mental Hygiene Clinic of Henry Street Settlement in an effort to bring mental health services to the low-income, multi-problem family in ways they may be able to use. This experiment tries to reduce their alienation and unfamiliarity by introducing a new learning experience—learning from going through a treatment process together, a process tailored to what they can understand and accept, rather than one that demands that they fit into the ways in which clinics operate.

The primary technique used is 'demonstration', in contrast with discussions alone, to help people reduce conflicts in intrafamilial relationships. It is combined with provision of concrete services. The essential elements in this technique are activity, intervention, and discussion.

* Published in *Social Work*, Vol. IX, No. 1, January 1964.

While treatment in the home is in some respects similar to the familiar technique in social casework practice of home visiting, it differs sharply in method and objectives. Among various points of similarity, both serve a diagnostic purpose in that they provide a picture of environmental influences and family interaction. Hence, insights are gained through observation and exploration. Both are used as follow-up when office appointments are not kept. The differences in this experiment are:

1. Treatment is shifted from the clinic to the home and takes place with continuity of regular appointments, systematically sustained.

2. In place of discussion with parents only, all members of the family are present; the social worker relates to all family members and their problems.

3. The social worker brings with him a variety of materials, such as arts and crafts media and simple games that all members can play. These serve as media through which conflicts between members are revealed as they participate in activity and as free wheeling responses occur.

4. As family members interact, the social worker either takes the role of catalyst to dramatize the particular conflict or intervenes to break into the destructive pattern as it occurs, and proceeds to demonstrate ways and means of settling the dispute, with all members participating in testing out and talking about the new methods.

The experiment was begun in August 1961 with a group of seven families selected for the reason that there was, in each, a concentration of socio-pathological problems in pervasive and extreme forms. These were families with children whose emotional disturbance was so severe that they could not be contained in any public school special class and who had therefore been suspended.

Without exception, the uncontrolled, impulsive acting-out behaviour in school was but a reflection of home conditions. Parents, severely deprived themselves, wanted good lives for their children but did not know how to accomplish this. They regarded the children's behaviour with resentment in view of the greater material advantages afforded them, and therefore were excessively restrictive and punitive as a means of control. They lived under one roof, in isolation, their only mode of communication being either verbal or physical abuse born of deep anger. Absent were demonstrable affection, structure, reasonable limits consistently applied, and other elements so necessary in child rearing for healthy growth.

The experiment was based on some broadly defined assumptions that grew out of an experience with this group the previous year, when efforts to provide mental health services in traditional ways had minimal results. The assumptions also represent the present hope of finding some answers to the discouragement prevalent in the field concerning the segment of population in the community, those who need mental health services the most can afford them the least, but, when they are offered, do not follow through when expected to conform to established patterns of clinic practice, i.e. appointments in the office and use of community resources.

The shifting of treatment from the clinic to the home was based upon the assumption that clinic appointments are alien to the experience and culture of this 'non-motivated' social class. They are alien to them because psychopathology is part and parcel of other social-economic-cultural problems and of their way of life. Under prevailing social conditions, many of which are admittedly unhealthy and which in our society tend to perpetuate themselves, normal efforts to adapt to these conditions produce what is called pathology. But, for the people who are trapped in these conditions is it pathological to rebel in the only ways they know how, lacking knowledge of any better ways? One has but to review their social histories and backgrounds to see and feel the heritage of 'pathology' running through one generation to another. It is as though pathology were imbibed with mother's milk. Is there any wonder that help for an emotional intra psychic problem alone has little or no meaning to people bedeviled by grim problems of survival?

A host of other considerations come to mind. Suspicion and fear born of ignorance, superstition, and misconceptions about mental health practically force rejection. Among the Puerto Rican population the word 'loco' is often muttered, accompanied by the appropriate gesture. Who among us wants to be thought crazy? The experiment set out to remedy this lack of knowledge, mindful, however, that this cannot be enough as long as conditions of poverty, unemployment, sub standard housing, and other social evils are still tolerated.

It was expected that bringing the service to these people in their own setting would reduce suspicion and convey an informal, friendly interest, divested of the authority of other agencies with which they are familiar—such as the courts, Department of Welfare, Housing Authority, school, and police—that compel compliance or mete out penalties. On the other hand, they should be less threatened by a friendly visit, since this is more in keeping with their own cultural standard. Increasing attention has been given to the role of fathers in the family constellation. Appointments planned at a time fathers are home includes them in a natural way.

If psychopathology is part and parcel of a way of life inseparable from social, cultural, and economic pathology, it cannot be treated successfully in isolation from other problems and from the members of the same family who affect each other and are contaminated in varying degrees by the same set of environmental influences. Moreover, to attempt to isolate one aspect (intra psychic) or to concentrate help on the one child who happens to be the offender of the moment increases parental defensiveness because they feel blamed. It is also not meaningful because of their distrust of help that, from their point of view, ignores the realities of their manifold problems. Therefore, the social worker should relate to all members of the family and be prepared to help with whatever problems individual members may have. This should pave the way for a trust of other community resources and should teach people how to use them.

The final assumption has relevance to questions of effectiveness of help, economy, and prevention. Familiar to the experience of many mental health clinics are the recidivist and the referral for treatment of a succession of children in the same family, as each in turn gets into trouble. It is also not uncommon to receive referrals for two or more children of the same family at the same time. This is not surprising if the crux of the many interrelated problems that impinge on all the children is not dealt with, and if long-term treatment of but one child is practiced. One might well ask how effective such efforts are—and how expensive in the aggregate.

The assumption is that 'treatment in the home' for these families should in the long run prove more economical for these reasons: Because problems are revealed in the living situation there is greater accuracy in diagnosis and the treatment process can be designed to reach the core of the problems, be initiated quickly, and progress more rapidly towards the resolution of conflict. Because all family members participate in the treatment, all can benefit and need not be referred individually, in succession. The first-hand knowledge obtained by this method makes it possible to catch other or related problems and prevent their development into more serious forms. Above all, time, money, and effort expended initially to reach the sources of problems for all family members should ensure more lasting improvement.

The selection of the technique of demonstration was made in the light of some of the common characteristics in this economically low social class. Conceptual or abstract thinking conveyed through words and phrases is beyond the capacities of this unsophisticated group, members of which are marginally educated, whose lives are a social and cultural wasteland, who act out anger and hostility, who have a low frustration tolerance and poor impulse control. Moreover, in the formative years of the parents and now of their children, words were and are used to manipulate and confuse others. These people do not comprehend the true meaning of words, have little faith in them, and are unable to carry out concepts defined by words alone. Verbal communication is therefore not only ineffectual but also subject to considerable distortion because there is no common frame of reference.

Doing or demonstrating what is needed should be more effective because the social worker's action, whether as catalyst or intervener, combined with discussion of the actual conflict situation as it is going on, means something to the family. It is meaningful because they see how the conflict develops and how it can be resolved without recourse to fights or beatings. It also eliminates the distortions that are common when conflict situations are reported after the fact and discussed in the office.

The use of play, utilizing arts and crafts materials and role-playing as the media by which treatment by demonstration takes place, was based upon two interrelated assumptions:

1. Just as children act out their problems in play therapy, so would their parents, who are immature, inadequate, confused, insecure, and in rivalry with each other and with their children. They function on the same emotional level as their children, have the same emotional needs, and respond to recognition of achievement in the same ways as their children.

2. As is commonly found among these families, the consequences of damaged parental personalities are emotional distance between the parents, between the parents and their children, and between the children. The many children, often unwanted, are not a source of pleasure. Parents do not know how to derive pleasure from or have fun with their children.

Play materials can provide this pleasure and should at the same time serve several objectives: teach the use of play materials for cultural enrichment, bridge gaps in communication, and alter emotional tones in communication as the activity permits teaching of reasonable limits, fair play, and how patience, tolerance, and respect for individual need and difference build better family relationships. Instead of discussions of failure, success is demonstrated as disputes are settled in which all members participate and all can feel a sense of accomplishment. To quote an old cliché, 'Nothing succeeds like success'.

Two case examples illustrate the method and the progress to date.

The M family, Puerto Rican, consists of thirteen persons living in five rooms in a low-cost housing project on a marginal income supplemented by the Department of Welfare. Both parents, in their early forty's, have minimal comprehension of English. Of the young children, one is in a residential treatment centre, a second was discharged a year ago from a state hospital and recently was re-admitted, and a third is mentally defective. Henry, aged ten, is in the settlement pilot project for boys suspended from school. Clinically he can be classified as borderline schizophrenic.

The home was always dirty and in a state of chaos due to constant fighting among the children over everything. Both parents either allowed unbridled behaviour or beat the children viciously and indiscriminately. A sibling of Henry, approaching, sixteen was ready to drop out of school, a six-year-old girl was always unkempt and withdrawn, doing poorly in school, the defective child vegetated, and the youngest, age two, was neglected and physically mistreated by everyone.

Mr M lived like a privileged boarder, keeping all his personal possessions locked in a closet. He never participated in the daily life of the family except to administer beatings. Mrs M, when not beating the children, acted like a disinterested bystander. Home was a shell, devoid of adequate furnishings and toys because 'they would only be broken'. Henry was obliged to sleep with the mentally ill brother, one year his senior, and with the defective child, both of whom interfered with his proper rest and contributed substantially to his problems. None of the objectives, including birth control, that had been set up by the clinic in the course of treatment the previous year had been realized.

Method of treatment. The social worker arranged his visits after the evening meal, bringing with him some simple games, including cards and clay. The children gathered around a table to play, but in the first few sessions the parents sat apart watching and the two-year-old was thrust aside. In the initial visits and play sessions the worker observed the spontaneous reactions of family members but did nothing else. When conflicts arose, the parents isolated the children or beat them.

Gradually both parents joined in the games and the worker began to include the two-year-old by showing him how to hold and use materials, indirectly demonstrating to the older children and to the parents how he could be taught. Frustrated on one occasion, he ran off screaming. The worker brought the child back, soothed him, and put him near his mother, whereupon he put his head in her lap. The worker then showed her how to play an appropriate game with him.

In activity, both parents manipulated, competed with the children, and cheated just as the children did. Gently, the worker introduced rules. In the weeks that followed, as rivalries, cheating, and angry outbursts occurred, the worker would stop, allow each to have his say, let them bring out and dramatize their feelings, and introduce concepts of fairness and respect for each other.

Before many sessions had passed, the family's interest in the worker's visits became clearly evident, for they were always ready on his arrival with table and places arranged, excitedly asking what they would do, and quickly settling down to activity. The worker supplemented evening visits with inclusion of one or more siblings in the group recreation programme (part of the treatment programme for the pilot project children) and with family bus trips provided by the settlement.

The apparent satisfaction with the visits enabled the parents to talk about other problems, which they brought up during the visit (for which time was set aside) or at the office, to which they were now willing to come. They talked first about sex and birth control. In the course of discussions it became evident that fears and ignorance accounted for their lack of action previously. The worker gathered information about various measures, accompanied the parents to possible sources of help, and in the process cleared away their misconceptions. They finally decided upon sterilization of the father, with which he went through.

A similar process of discussion, with the worker accompanying parents and child each step of the way from referral through the complicated processing in various agencies, eventuated in placement of the defective child in a state school and re-admission of the mentally ill child to the state hospital. The sixteen-year-old girl's plan to drop out of school was brought up and she then confided her ambition to become a nurse. Psychological and vocational tests were administered and plans worked out for her to remain in school. A Big Sister was provided for the six-year-old, and the parents were now willing to have the younger child enrolled in the after-school play school, thus relieving some of the pressures on the mother.

Progress. After approximately ten months of intensive work there is some tangible evidence of beginning change. Mrs M feels less harassed and attends to household tasks. Hence, the home is cleaner and beginning to look more inviting, having some decorative objects. With the defective and mentally ill children in institutions, there is less crowding and less general chaos. Increasingly, parents and children have begun to talk out their grievances, hence there are fewer tantrums, less fighting among the siblings, and less frequent parental beatings.

The children attending play school are learning how to conform to reasonable discipline and, in the process, learning that the adult world and authority can be understanding. They are also enriching themselves educationally and culturally. The six-year-old girl has changed from an uncommunicative, unkempt, unhappy child to a responsive, spirited youngster. All the children are more alert, more responsive, show more interest in learning, and are doing better in school. The parents are beginning to exert some controls without recourse to beating. Emotional distance has lessened and the general home atmosphere is less hostile.

Perhaps the best signs of progress are two events that occurred recently: For the first time in their children's lives, the parents made a birthday party for one of them (Henry), to which the worker was invited. Games were played, refreshments served, pictures taken, and fun had by all. In a second instance, Mrs M on her own initiative called the clinic to ask help in arranging dental care for the school-age children.

The C's are a Chinese family living in a crowded, four-room slum tenement. Mr C is fifteen years older than his wife and there are four school-age children, the oldest twelve and the youngest six. Tom, the nine-year-old, is in the settlement's pilot project. He had violent, uncontrollable temper outbursts, during which he would run out of the school building. His ten-year-old brother Danny was released a few months ago from a state hospital and, except for his re-admission to school, there was little follow-up by the after-care clinic in assessing his problems or needs in readjustment to the family and community.

Mr C works out of the city and is home only on his day off. Mrs C also works, so that the children are unsupervised for many hours during the day. Parental resentment towards each other found its outlet either in their running away from each other or in explosions of violent outbursts against the children.

Typical forms of discipline used by the parents were to isolate the children when they got into fights, beat them in explosive fits of anger, or tell them that Danny was crazy and should be left alone. When Danny broke another child's possessions he was not disciplined. He was also allowed special privileges. When he showed anger he was promised gifts, which were forgotten when he calmed down. These devices naturally contributed to resentment among the children and to Danny's withdrawal from the family and from the community. From sexual relations to the way chairs were allocated, the pattern of avoidance of contact in order to avoid difficulty was maintained.

Method of treatment. The worker's visits were planned at a time when all family members were present, which was before the evening meal. The children were always around the kitchen table ready to begin a game or to work with clay. In the first few sessions Mr C would sit near by but not participate except to criticize or correct the children, and Mrs C would continue preparing the evening meal, with one eye on the table to see what was going on. During this period, too, considerable attention was diverted towards Danny, who, in keeping with the parental discipline of isolating him, hung back and would not come into the room. He finally came in after some tentative moves.

In the games or other activities Danny did quite well in learning to share materials and adult attention while the worker was present. Yet, as the time approached to terminate the session, he would invariably provoke one of the other children. During one session he claimed he won a game of cards, although Tom was the real winner. Mrs C immediately pushed the winning cards to Danny in order to avert the tantrum she anticipated. Tom, furious, ran off in tears. Enlisting the parents' help, the worker brought Tom back, gently but firmly, and the issue was discussed before everybody. As this was clarified, other grievances between the brothers were brought out. Danny had broken a table that Tom had made in the settlement wood-shop and proudly taken home. The parents claimed it was beyond repair. The worker had the table brought in, looked over, and repaired there and then, with Danny's help.

In succeeding weeks, incidents such as these and others typical in the lives of children who are in rivalry and angry with each other were either observed or reported during the activity sessions. Each time the worker would encourage each to tell his version and bring out his feelings, and each time the grievance or dispute would either be settled to everybody's satisfaction or it would be evident that angry feelings were in better control.

Mrs C, who previously had said she could not understand or speak English, not only spoke more often in English but began to participate in the games and in other activities, showing quite a flair for original design. Mr C, although still overtly directive, also joined in and began to play with the children. Both parents responded with pleasure to recognition of their efforts.

Progress. After seven months of treatment Danny, formerly an isolate and shunned, began to act out his feelings. Although this disturbed the parents somewhat, they admitted that he now seldom lost his temper and was easier to handle in the home. Seeing this much improvement in him, they allowed the social worker to bring some of the settlement's group workers to the home to meet them and to hear from the workers how activities would benefit Danny. The parents then permitted him to join the settlement's after-school activity programme and to participate in some of the pilot project activities with Tom, including group treatment sessions. Tom learned ways of standing up for himself in place of violent temper outbursts and running away.

Mr and Mrs C are now taking time to listen to grievances when they arise and trying to settle them, rather than lashing out with a beating. There is less violent fighting, with consequent improvement in the home atmosphere.

The contrast in relationship can be illustrated by two incidents that occurred about six months apart. Six months ago, when Mr C was called by the teacher in the clinic's school to prevent Tom from running out of the building in a rage, he began to beat Tom the moment he saw him, and was stopped only by the clinic director's intervention. Recently, the director met Tom and his father on the street, walking hand in hand. When Tom did not immediately respond politely to the director's greeting, Mr C quietly asked him to do so. Formerly this offence would have been the occasion for rage and a beating.

The two case examples illustrate progress that is by no means spectacular, but which in a period of approximately seven to ten months indicates beginning change, change also observed in the remaining five project children and in their families.

In describing progress the use of adjectives such as 'less' fighting and 'more' parental effort implies change that is a matter of degree, that is relative and in contrast to attitudes and behaviour prior to the experiment. It also implies change that is in flux and thus subject to relapse. Therefore, a much longer period of work with the same method is needed to indicate whether these changes can be strengthened and firmly imbedded as a new way of life among these families. There

E

is no intent to imply, however, that this method can succeed with all low-income, multi-problem families, or that all low-income, multi-problem families are the same. On the contrary, despite some common characteristics mentioned, there is recognition of a wide range of individual differences among this group, so that no one method or technique can be applied to all or be successful with all. This experiment shows merely that some families commonly classified as 'low income, multi-problem' appear to be responding to the method described.

Only highlights and condensed versions of a multitude of variegated responses to what was done in activity sessions have been presented. The materials used were not important in themselves except as they served as media for activity to catch interest, afford pleasure, and work out problems. For example, another psychiatric social worker dealing with a similar 'hard-to-reach' family hit on the medium of a tool chest, which he brought with him to the home after some initial visits during which he had observed broken furniture, broken toys, and the like. In this family the mother and six young children took turns during mealtime in sitting on the only functioning chair in the kitchen. As the worker proposed and then went ahead with some minor repairs, the children before long became curious, interested, and finally joined in the activity. Other services and problem-solving then proceeded as a matter of course.

What really has been accomplished so far, and to what extent do the assumptions hold up? Is there any correlation between treatment in the homes and the improvement noted in all the project children?

The stimulus for change or improvement was imposed by external means in a repetitive, consistent way, in order to bring about some environmental change. The intrapsychic or unconscious was not directly touched. The effectiveness of such improvement could therefore be questioned by colleagues who believe real change can come only from within the personality.

Whatever its shortcomings, can there be much dispute over the possibility that environmental change may be all that can be accomplished with certain people, given our present limited knowledge, tools, and resources? Also, is it not possible that environmental change can lead to inner change? If something is done often enough it eventually becomes habitual. Showing how something needs to be done is concrete and therefore more easily understood, since family members can see and do, and feel the gratification of immediate success, rather than being told what should be done and left to do it alone when they do not know how. Following this, the recognition of accomplishment and ensuing feelings of importance as human beings led them to ask for and use help for other pressing problems, for which concrete services were given.

Therefore, shifting treatment to the homes did enable these families to use help and did bring about beginning improvement. Concrete services then provided other media to teach and to share with them satisfying experiences in the use of other community resources they so desperately needed.

Is their apathy and their indifference towards social and authoritative agencies so surprising when one thinks about the bureaucratic procedures characteristic of so many agencies—procedures that are often mystifying and frustrating even to professional groups? Telephoning, filling in forms, fragmentation of services, innumerable trips and waiting only to be told to return another time, meeting well-intentioned but harassed workers who are brusque and impersonal, who often quote directives or regulations that are so codified as to defy anyone's intelligence—all these are incomprehensible, especially to people who are not proficient in the language, are unfamiliar with our customs, cannot leave babies at home to travel long distances, and who achieve no satisfaction. An agency represents to them a monstrous machine of which they are afraid. Teaching them how to use community resources by sharing the experience can reduce their fears.

To return to the external stimulus for change, the technique of demonstration should not be construed as 'taking over' the parental role, or control, or responsibility because it contains elements of direction or even manipulation. Nor does it necessarily follow that once the external stimulus is removed families will revert to former patterns, and that therefore change is superficial and temporary. On the contrary, the treatment process demands from the worker the utmost in alertness and sensitivity to undercurrents of parental feelings of resentment or threat to what they may feel to be abrogation of their control. Despite their inadequacies (perhaps because of them) they are apt to withdraw if they feel their 'rights' as parents pre-empted. Mindful of this, the worker does not plunge into directing. To begin with, he tells them he is there to learn what their difficulties are and to see if with his help they can work them out. There is often patient waiting, just being there. The worker verbalizes feelings the family may have about what he is doing and to what end. He must judge their readiness to move on, pace, time, and measure how much and how far he will intervene and direct, but he is always reassuring by setting straight in their minds (parents and children alike) that the parents hold the authority and the control. When such fears are truly allayed, and participation of the parents gained, the change can become part of daily living. Hence, demonstration as a technique in treatment was understandable and had meaning for these families. It also bridged some gaps in communication and improved family relationships.

Recognizable in this experiment are some parallels with family casework, at least in terms of focus on the family and the combination of concrete services with efforts to reach more problems and build upon whatever strengths can be detected. However, in working with this group, family service agencies are apt too often to seek the 'motivated' client and to attempt modification of patterns of behaviour through some level of insight therapy.

Perhaps the best that can be put forth on the question of economy and prevention is the consideration that in acting on all the problems of all family members simultaneously there takes place the breaking up of maladjustment or pathology in the incipient stage when patterns of behaviour can be reversible. Thus the individual is enabled to move ahead in growth to cope better with problems with fewer crippling symptoms; there is also less interference from the impinging pathology of other family members. In the two illustrations given, the pathology of other siblings had a direct bearing upon the difficulties of the project children, and this is also true of the other five project children. The extent to which this is significant can be judged by the fact that, for the case load of seven children and their families, sixty-nine individuals, including close relatives, received services of one kind or another during the same period.

Treatment in the homes and the technique of demonstration can be further evaluated by the research findings on the relationship between progress in the parents and improvement in the five children who have been constant in the project. Quoting from the research:

As has been stated, it was everyone's impression that both day-to-day fluctuations and more stable changes in the children's behaviour often directly paralleled vicissitudes in the home. Everyone connected with the project felt that the children benefited from the changes in the family milieu effected by the 'Treatment in the Homes' programme. We wanted, however, to go beyond impressions and determine whether or not more objective evidence supported our view.

If, we reasoned, treatment in the home was instrumental in the children's behaviour, there should be a positive correlation between degree of improvement in the child and parents. If treatment in the home was ineffectual, one would expect no correlation between child and parental progress.

Each child was periodically rated by project teacher, social workers, recreational group workers, on a five-point behavioural rating scale.[1] On degree of improvement or worsening taken together these ratings provided a quantitative index of each child's progress or lack of progress. The parents of the children were independently ranked on degree of progress in treatment by the social worker who carried out treatment in the homes of these families.

Table 1. Ratings on Degree of Progress of Parents and Children.

Social Workers' Ratings of Parents	Quantitative Index for Children
Most improvement	
Mrs T	GT
Mrs Sl	LSl
Mr and Mrs C	LC
Mr S	WS
Mr M	HM
Mrs S	
Mrs M	
Least improvement	

[1] There are five points on the scale, each of which was assigned a quantative value: 'no improvement' (0), 'some improvement' (+1), 'marked improvement' (+2), 'some worsening' (−1), 'marked worsening' (−2). This rating scale was only one of many instruments for measurement of progress. Others were projective tests, achievement tests, classroom observations, anecdotal reports, interviews, and other rating scales.

The results of these ratings can be seen (in Table 1). On the left are social workers' ratings of the parents from 'most' to 'least' (improvement). On the right, the children are ranked on the basis of the quantitative index 'most' to 'least' . . .

As can be seen from (Table 1) (by comparing rank positions of corresponding initials in parents and children columns), there is an extremely close correlation between parental progress as evaluated by the social worker and children's progress as reflected by the quantitative index derived from the behaviour rating scale.

It should be emphasized that Table 1 shows *relative* position only. Thus, for example, although HM and his parents, one of the cases described earlier, are in the lowest positions *relative to the others*, it does not mean that they fail to show progress. On the contrary, HM, who was our sickest child and most refractory to therapeutic attempts, showed important changes, although to a lesser degree than did the other children. HM's family environment, which in some regards was the most confused and disturbed of all our families, did nevertheless improve.

We are not suggesting that the above reflects a cause and effect relationship, since correlations indicate association between variables without revealing the nature or even the presence of a cause and effect relationship. But the results are consistent without observations that the 'Treatment in the Homes' did effect concrete changes in the way parents responded to and dealt with their children, and that these changes are reflected in the improved behaviour of the children.

The results of the second year of the experiment, ending June 30, 1963, may be of interest to readers. Indicated in the preceding discussion of the first year was the realization of beginning change that could be subject to relapse. In the M family, for example, when treatment was interrupted for a few months because of the absence of a social worker, relapse into former patterns was to be expected (and actually occurred) in view of the fragile nature of beginning improvement. However, in the second year only a few visits were required to re-establish the family on the road towards progress. During the balance of the year the family made substantial advances.

The same rate of progress was made by all but one family in the study, in which damage in the mother proved irreversible. All the children in the project were returned to public schools in September 1963 and all are thus far making satisfactory adjustments. In short, the close correlation found at the end of the first year between the rates of improvement in the home and in the children was conclusive at the end of the second year. The striking correspondence between parental progress and the children's progress left no doubt of the validity of the treatment techniques used.

5

CHILDREN'S PLAY AS A CONCERN OF FAMILY CASEWORKERS*

PAULINE SHAPIRO

THE importance of children's play has long been recognized by social workers as well as by educationists and therapists. Nursery groups, play centres and more recently play parks and adventure playgrounds are provisions for children's play that owe much to the concern and activities of social workers. Yet these are all organizations for play outside the children's own homes. Apart from the distribution of children's toys by various charities at Christmas, I do not know of any organized effort concerned with the individual play of young children in their own homes.

I have been led to reflect on what now seems to me this gap in the social services as a result of arranging child care students' practical work, which for nine years included a study of large families. The beginning of this study has been described elsewhere.[1] For our present purposes it is enough to say that each student was introduced to two large families[2] selected as a contrast. In the one the mother was able to 'cope' to the extent of providing loving care and control of her children and of achieving at least minimal material standards, in the other, the 'non-coping' mother might show affection to some or all of her children but was usually unable to control them or to achieve minimal material standards, her family thus becoming the concern of many social agencies. Each student visited two such families at least weekly during the academic sessions and was required to write social histories and detailed narrative accounts of all visits.

Almost immediately I became aware of a sharp differentiation

* Published in *Case Conference*, Vol. IX, No. 7, January 1963.
[1] Pauline C. Shapiro, 'The Search for a "Norm" in Home Life', *The British Journal of Psychiatric Social Work*, Vol. II, No. 6, June 1952.
[2] After the initial stages a 'large family' came to mean one where there were at least five children of school age or under.

between the 'copers' and the 'non-copers' in respect of their children's play. Students complained that though they could learn about family background, children's early histories and so on, in the coping families, it was impossible to elicit such information in the non-coping families. Quiet discussion took place with the coping parents because their children were happily engaged in play and would return to their playthings once the novelty of a strange visitor had worn off. In the 'non-copers' homes, on the other hand, there was no provision for indoor play; usually there was pandemonium—coaxing and slapping, often ending in money for lollies or sweet biscuits from the corner shop, which only brought a brief respite. The suggestion that students should take to these homes simple playthings, such as paper and crayons or plasticine, produced remarkable results out of all proportion to the equipment. Respite became prolonged and relationships, at least temporarily, peaceful. I recall one family with an energetic obstreperous three-year-old, a terror to the student and to his mother, who believed him to be uncontrollable and destructive. The long winter months lay ahead in cramped surroundings. By good fortune the father worked in a building yard which contained long pieces of squared wood. After he had been encouraged to cut some of these into varying lengths to make an assortment of strong blocks for his small son, there was a decided improvement in family relationships— and in the attitude of the student visiting the family.

It was therefore no surprise when the recorded material came to be analysed, to find that, with hardly any exceptions, the 'copers' provided for their children's play needs and the 'non-copers' did not. This does not mean merely the presence or absence of toys. On the contrary, the 'non-copers' were often extravagant in buying conspicuous objects—tricycles, prams, over-large dolls or animals—for display at Christmas. But in their homes there was a complete lack of play material for constructive and imaginative use, and even worse, a lack of understanding or tolerance of children's play needs.

I will illustrate this contrast by some excerpts from the students' narrative records, beginning with a representative sample of the 'copers'. These extracts are unchanged except for the names.

The Palmers

The living room is a comfortable room. When the children are at school during the day it appears clean and very tidy; however, as soon as they return it becomes littered with pieces of paper and toys . . . I said to Mrs P that George (14 years) had shown me one or two of the comics he had drawn and I thought they were very good. She said that he did nothing else but draw. I asked if he had drawn them completely by himself or whether he had copied and traced some of them. She said that he drew them all by himself and made up the story.

(Ten children from 16 years to 5 months. Terrace house of five rooms, no garden, no modern conveniences.)

This home was remarkable for the ample provision of play material and the mother's tolerance of the mess it made in spite of her good material standards. This resulted in the happy activities of the children and the encouragement of their talents and creativity. George gave the student who visited this family one of his own 'comics', neatly hand-written with crayoned illustrations, which showed vivid imagination, albeit of a lurid kind, and considerable ability in drawing.

The Watkins

When two children were clamouring for something to do Mrs W offered to get them chalk. I looked after them for a few minutes, reading a comic to Linda while she went for some chalk and then she fetched down a sizeable easel and blackboard.

(Six children from 8 years to 1½ years. Courtyard house, one living room, two bedrooms. No modern conveniences.)

This is a young couple who both enjoy playing with their children while maintaining reasonable discipline. The variety of play material keeps the six young children well occupied in a very restricted space.

The Weavers

Mrs Weaver, who comes from a village in Ireland, mentions how lucky she was as a child to have had so much space to play in, with so few restrictions, and how she wishes her own children could know the same freedom . . . On another occasion I remarked how much the children must enjoy themselves as they are always playing. Mrs Weaver thought it was even more important than food with them, as it was often a job to get them in to meals and she regretted they didn't have more space to play in, but perhaps they would when the new house materialized.

(Six children from 11 years to 10 months. Courtyard house, living room and kitchen, three small bedrooms. No modern conveniences.)

The mother was herself one of a large family (ten children) for whom she still retains great affection. She makes the most of the tiny rooms of the present accommodation by lighting fires in both living room and kitchen throughout the winter and giving the children the free run of the ground floor.

The Nortons

Patricia (nearly 3 years) came in from the scullery and demanded 'Pins and clothes'. She was busy hanging out her 'washing'. She thoroughly enjoys playing like this and is provided with a few small articles and some water and a chair to stand on at the sink. Mrs N seems very patient with her and acceded to the demand for 'more clothes'. She thinks this is the kind of play that should be encouraged by a mother. Patricia meanwhile had got one of David's nappies he sometimes has at nights, and was trying *very* hard to put it on her soft doll, grasping its legs at the ankles and lifting them as one would do to a baby. She was very serious about the whole business and I noticed Mrs N let her get on with it but made practical suggestions such as 'Fold it double and it will be easier, Pat.'
(Five children from 11 to 2 years. Courtyard house of five small rooms, no modern conveniences.)

Mrs Norton is an excellent housewife and devoted mother who responds intuitively to her children's needs (the student marvelled how Mrs N always did the right thing without reference to any textbook; e.g. she put her two pre-school children to rest at different times of the day so that each could enjoy a period of her undivided attention). She approves of her little daughter's play as a preparation for adult life. Though psycho-analytic interpretation might be different, the result is the same—a little girl absorbed in play, developing skills and coming to terms with her feelings.

The Francis Family

We went to the end of the garden where there was an accumulation of 'treasures'—a small plastic bath, a jam jar full of dirt, an enamel bowl, a rod on wheels and one or two broken Dinky toys. Mary said she was going to make me some dinner and put some dirt on a Dinky lorry, spread it over carefully with a knife, and then shook it off deliberately before handing it to me and insisting that I ate every bit. My pretence at eating it amused the children tremendously, and the whole performance was repeated about a dozen times, with exactly the same ritual and no lessening of amusement.
(Six children from 6 years to 3 months. Five-roomed terraced house with garden. No modern conveniences.)

This is one of many illustrations that could have been taken from the records of 'coping' families of a proper respect for children's 'treasures', which are so often household utensils and other junk.

Let us now turn to a similar number of examples taken from the records of the 'non-copers'.

The Clancy Family

Mrs Clancy was full of the wonderful Christmas they had. One of her sisters provided their Christmas dinner and her brother, home on leave from Japan, brought toys for all the children. I was shown these toys, which included bears and a caterpillar which moved when wound up. Mrs C had bought all the girls 'walky-talky' dolls . . . A visitor had called from the *Sunday Pictorial* and brought six books and a toy motor-car. It was the first time I had seen toys in the room and I thought it such a pity that the children were not allowed to play with them. Most of the toys were propped on the mantelpiece and the books were kept in the cupboard. Mrs C told me she was determined they should not get damaged. I looked at a picture book which had stand-up pictures, showing them to Doreen (4) and Geoffrey (3), and Mrs C shouted at the children every time they touched the pictures.
(Seven children from 9 years to 11 months, mother again pregnant. Back-to-back courtyard house. One kitchen-living room, two bed-rooms. No modern conveniences.)

This family previously lived in lodgings and have been evicted from their first home. The father is seldom at work, the mother is dull and uncertain in her attitudes to her children, one of whom serves as a scapegoat for much of her aggression and despair; at times she ignores the children's 'naughtiness', at times she will bellow at them and clout them. The standards are far below minimal standards, the rent is again in arrears, and the cooker has been removed.

The Sutcliff Family

John (a backward child of 4 years) spends most of his time while I am there standing by his mother's knee. There are normally no toys in sight and he either plays with his mother's legs or with odd bits of material he finds—a dirty napkin, for example—and one afternoon just stood on the hearth (no fireguard) masturbating.

Mark (2½ years) is fond of imaginative games in the absence of toys. I open my hand and he pretends to take something out of it and carries it across the room and puts it down, then he picks it up, brings it to me and puts it in my hand. I close my hand for a second and then open it and the same thing happens again. This will be repeated at least a dozen times. Sometimes his mother will tell him to be a bogy man. He puts his hands above his head and shakes them . . . Usually he is very quiet. He and Peter hardly ever laugh . . . I have seen some soft toys in the house, dolls and animals, but nothing which might stimulate the children to create something such as bricks, clay and plasticine. (Six children from 12 years to one month. Accommodation, kitchen-living room, two bedrooms and two attics, yard. No modern conveniences.)

This mother is depressed and apathetic, showing little interest in her children and none in household affairs. Marital relations are strained and material standards very poor indeed. The student visiting Mrs Sutcliff comments: 'Mrs S seems completely dissatisfied . . . she dislikes the house where they now live, says she has no friends, thinks that she has too many children already and fears that she may be pregnant again.'

The Benn Family

There appeared to be no toys for the children to play with, but they played among themselves, often jumping on and off the furniture. Sometimes when Mrs Benn would be talking to me, she would break off and start talking to and playing with the children by perhaps climbing on the table or rolling on the sofa with them. There was an immature excitement about it. (Eight children from 13 years to $1\frac{1}{2}$ years; four children, including twins, are under five. Council house, two living rooms, three bedrooms and bathroom.)

The dilapidated condition of the Benn's house is in marked contrast to the possibilities of the house. Mr Benn escapes to the pub and does nothing to help with the children or to keep the house in repair or the garden tended. Mrs Benn, who married at seventeen, has known good standards in domestic service and maintained them in the early days of her marriage. Circumstances have overwhelmed her, both in her relations with her husband and in the increasing size of her family. She is not unintelligent, but would be regarded as irresponsible in the way she lives from hand to mouth and allocates her inadequate 'wages'.

The Mills Family

It is noticeable that there are never any toys for the younger children to play with. They are expected to be quiet but there is nothing to occupy them. Marion ($2\frac{1}{2}$ years) will spend an hour sitting

on the head of the sofa pulling at the curtains, Paul ($3\frac{1}{2}$ years) is throwing a piece of stick aimlessly about and Geoffrey ($1\frac{1}{2}$ years) is vainly trying to pull himself put of his pram. Mrs Mills is continually telling them to 'stop it' but it is always ineffective.
(Seven children from 14 to $1\frac{1}{2}$. Four rooms. No garden.)

Again there were good standards and much happier relations while there were only three children. There has been a rapid deterioration with the birth of the last four children at almost yearly intervals. After a very difficult confinement with Marion, Mrs Mills was advised to have no more children. At forty, she is now an ailing woman, constantly complaining about her symptoms and the young children's 'naughtiness'.

The Akbar Family

They seem to have almost nothing to play with and what they have is most unsuitable for them. K. and J. (4 and 3 years) were given snakes and ladders to play with and a very difficult puzzle. I have not seen them with any toys or materials. It is very natural for them, as a result of this, to become restless and quarrelsome.
(Five children from 5 years to 5 months. Courtyard house of four rooms. No modern conveniences.)

Mrs Akbar is a young woman of twenty-four, married to a middle-aged Moslem who works long hours of overtime. Five years of marriage, bearing a baby each year, have left her bitterly frustrated, with little maternal feeling or understanding of her children.

It will have been noted that the housing of these large families is very similar, but whereas the 'coping' mothers make the most of restricted space and in different ways satisfy some of their children's play needs, the 'non-copers' do not. The brief notes about the families indicate the intuitive response of the 'copers' to their children's needs, and the amount of poor physical and mental health and disturbed relationships militating against such benign response in the families of the 'non-copers'. Such conditions seem to be basic to much of the malfunctioning of these homes.

It has therefore been logical for social workers to concentrate their efforts with 'problem' families on the poor physical conditions, the muddles of mismanagement and strained relationships of the adults, in the correct assumption that their amelioration would automatically improve the lot of the children. Experience since the war has shown, however, that intensive casework of this kind with 'problem' families is always slow and often uncertain in its results, and may constitute a holding operation until the children grow older. The Family Service Units have recently extended their efforts in direct work with the children themselves, bringing them to their Centres for play and helping to arrange holidays for them, while a close link with day nurseries, nursery schools, play centres and clubs of the area has been a traditional feature of their work. In this connection, the experimental nursery school for children of large families established in Cardiff in 1960 by the Society of Friends, is of great interest and its findings will be eagerly awaited.[1] The recent developments of play parks and adventure playgrounds, to which the pioneering efforts of Lady Allen of Hurtwood[2] and others have contributed so much, and the thought now being given to play provision for children in high flats,[3] show an encouraging recognition of the importance of children's play.

Yet, as I have pointed out, these developments all provide for children's play outside their own homes. They still touch only the fringe in meeting the need of the many children of 'non-copers'. For pre-school children, where the need is greatest, nursery groups are thin on the ground and, with the exception of the Cardiff experiment, seldom enrol the children of large families. Throughout nine years of studying such families I cannot recall a single one whose pre-school children attended a nursery group. Though this situation can be contemplated with some equanimity in the homes of the 'copers' it must surely cause disquiet on behalf of children of 'non-copers'. If one subscribes, as I do, to the theory of play suggested by Erik Erikson 'that the child's play is the infantile form of the human ability to deal with experience by creating model situations and to master reality by experience and planning',[4] can one doubt that this lack of play material in the homes of 'non-copers' is damaging to their children's whole development, particularly in the early years? These children, encompassed by problems of relationship, have little opportunity to work through them in play and nothing to stimulate their mental growth, while their mothers' difficulties in 'coping' are greatly exacerbated by young children around them with nothing to do. This vicious circle is made more vicious by the inclement weather of this country, with the necessity of spending so much time indoors.

I suggest, therefore, that family caseworkers might usefully give

[1] Dr Harriet Wilson, 'An Experimental Nursery School', Child Care, Vol. XVI, No. 2, April 1962.
[2] Lady Allen of Hurtwood, Design for Play, The Housing Centre Trust, London, 1962.
[3] J. Maizels and E. White, 'Two to Five in High Flats', Housing Review, January-February 1962, Vol. II, No. 1, pp. 23-26.
[4] Erik H. Erikson, Childhood and Society, Imago Press, London, N.D., p. 159.

more thought to young children's play needs within the homes of the families they visit. They should be concerned not only with the provision of simple play material and the imaginative use of household 'junk' but also with an approach to children's play needs which might involve the mother indirectly through example and interest. Maybe directly too. The mothers, perhaps released from apathy by the fireside, eased in their problems of disciplining the children and freer to do some household chores, might also come to enjoy their children's play and in so doing, find some relief from their own pressing personal problems. As a corollary, those concerned with training social workers (and health visitors, too, for here is a fruitful field of co-operation) might give more space in their curricula to teaching about practical ways of meeting children's play needs at different stages of development, in addition to their more academic instruction about the significance of play.

In my mind's eye I picture future maternity and child welfare centres giving prominence, equal to that already assigned to dried milks and orange juice, to simple play material for young children (at reduced prices), holding 'make do and mend' classes for toys as well as clothes, and sending out their health visitors as knowledgeable about, and as interested in, young children's mental food as they have long been in their physical nutrition; charities staggering their distribution of toys, so that there is no longer the present plethora at Christmas and starvation for the rest of the year; and social workers co-operating with such charities so that they think in terms of play material rather than toys, and distribution becomes geared to indvidual need.

Is such a picture merely fanciful? Perhaps Mrs Weaver was wiser than most of us when she said that children's play was even more important to them than food.

6

DAVID AND HIS MOTHER*

NOEL K. HUNNYBUN

THE following is an account of joint casework with a mother and her little son with the object of helping to restore a damaged relationship. It is one of several cases with whom I have worked on somewhat similar lines. It repsesents a limited piece of work since it was confined to those aspects of the mutual problem which mother and son presented to me during the first and subsequent sessions. As will be seen, I never penetrated far below the surface.

David, aged two years and seven months, was referred by a health visitor who was distressed by the unhappy relationship between the child and his mother. The health visitor described David as 'a little terror'. My first meeting with David and his mother took place in a maternity and child welfare centre some distance from the child guidance clinic where, as a matter of convenience, I sometimes met parents for preliminary interviews, thus saving them at least one long journey to the clinic. Actually, the psychiatrist never saw David for, after hearing what had taken place at my first meeting with child and mother, he suggested that I should give them direct help without his intervention. He would hold a watching brief over the case.

On the day of the mother's first appointment, as I was saying goodbye to another mother, I saw a young woman advancing with speed up the pathway leading to the centre, pushing a small boy in a go-cart. Released from it, the child came into the hall, with reluctant steps and bowed head, looking the picture of misery. The mother appeared to be very heated and said angrily: 'I don't know whether it's David, his father or me which is the trouble.' I invited them into my room, setting a chair beside mine for the mother and placing some toys on the floor. But David stood at the door, in what appeared to be mute misery, while his mother burst forth with tales of his misdeeds and

* Published in *The British Journal of Psychiatric Social Work*, Vol. VI, No. 3, 1962.

the hardships of her lot in having so naughty a child. At the end of this recital David slowly and silently entered the room and finally edged himself between our feet. After a few minutes, during which he sat quite still between us, I put my hand down and touched his head. He looked up with a most engaging smile to which I responded. I then said that, as he knew, his mother had been telling me about some of the things he had been doing which she did not like, such as pulling off the table-cloth at mealtimes, so that everything got broken, adding that I did not think he would always want to do things like this. David then moved nearer to me and I continued to talk with him, letting him know in a very simple way that I was well aware that he and his mother were at odds. While this was going on the mother's anger seemed to be cooling a little. However, it became evident that she was somewhat resentful of the attention being paid to her 'naughty' child when she said rather crossly that David 'loved to be made a fuss of'. She then enlarged again on the badness of his behaviour, giving several examples, which showed that many of her complaints centred round the kind of mischief that might be expected of any normal small boy of his age. Her complaints and her behaviour vividly demonstrated a state of tension and unhappiness between her and the little boy. Having given vent to some of her feelings, she could then tell me about the family. She said that David was the elder of two children, the younger, Julie, was not a year old and the father was a chef. She then talked a little about her own family, which consisted of three girls; she was the eldest, the youngest now aged eight was fifteen years her junior, and had always been utterly spoilt, whereas she and her next sister had been brought up very strictly. The mother then spoke of the nice home she and her husband had made and of which she was very proud and how David was wrecking it. The mother seemed oppressed by the amount of work she had to do now that she had two children, saying, rather guiltily I thought, that in consequence she rarely had time to play with David, though she always managed to give him a good cuddle at bedtime. As his mother talked David still remained seated between us on the floor until, encouraged by me, he gradually made some tentative moves towards some trains at which he was making longing eyes, but he did not feel sufficiently reassured to play with them until I put them well within his reach. I then asked the mother whether she and David would come again next week to see whether I could help both with their difficulties. To this she readily agreed.

When they paid their next visit, David was much happier and more

F

confident. He came straight into my room and played happily and constructively with the toys, showing considerable skill in manipulating the trains which he eventually pushed around the floor with much enjoyment. I played with him a little which he seemed to enjoy, but I made it clear that the time we had together would be shared between him and his mother. This fair sharing of my time presented, both on this occasion and subsequently, some difficulties to both because of the mother's need to absorb my time and attention by telling me of her hardships in having to combine domestic duties with the care of her two lively children who, as she said, were so demanding. I began to see, as she talked, that her own demandingness might well be one of the difficulties between herself and them. I wondered also whether her present impatience with David stemmed, in part at least, from her feelings about her own little sister who, as the mother had told me, had been so indulged and spoilt. I could see too how difficult it was for this mother to modify her high standards of home care, which she was evidently trying to maintain against, I imagined, pretty heavy odds. This seemed to be illustrated by her constant need, while the three of us were together, to check David's play by telling him to be careful of the toys and not to make a mess. Seeing her difficulty in allowing him to play freely, I pointed out that actually I was pleased that he was liking the toys so much and was playing so happily with them. She accepted this fairly graciously and then became a little less restraining. At this point, I told the mother that I had discussed David with the psychiatrist and that it had been decided that, if she so wished, attendance at the child guidance clinic could be waived, anyway for the time being, so that she and David and I could continue to sort out some of the difficulties that existed between them. She seemed glad to accept this arrangement and the session ended with all of us helping to put the toys back in their appointed place.

From then on the mother and David attended the centre, with few absences, over a period of six and a half months. I found the sessions very enjoyable though exacting for it was often difficult to be aware of what was taking place within this tri-partite relationship. At one of the early sessions I said they each wanted to absorb my time and attention and explained that we would have to try to work things out so that each got fair shares. I also told David that he could play both in my room and in the waiting room, reminding him, however, that there were some things in the centre which belonged to other people and these I could not let him use. We had a look together at these tempting objects, which included a sterilizer, a mop and pail, and some other bits of the nurses' equipment. I did not expect that David would always resist the lure of these tantalizing things. Neither did he, but his infringements of these 'rules' gave me a chance of dealing, at first hand, with his anger when frustrated. There were battles at times and, for the first week or two, I stood aside so that the mother could deal with them, fearing that if I interfered before she had gained some confidence in me, I should inevitably be cast in the role of the mother's own mother, who allegedly had been so indulgent with the mother's youngest sister. After a few sessions I asked the mother whether she would let me take over the management of David while at the centre. I knew that this request might arouse the mother's hostility and increase her existing sense of failure, especially if David were to be responsive to my control and management. Yet I decided on this course in the hope that opportunities would arise of helping the mother to discover new ways of managing her very mischievous and often rebellious little boy. She, having agreed to my request, rarely intervened, though at times her patience was sorely tried.

Some interesting situations then ensued. Once, for instance, while the mother and I were deeply involved in a discussion, I became aware of an ominous silence. When I went in search of David I found him busily engaged in plastering all the waiting room chairs with a mixture of baby powder and methylated spirit taken from the nurses' cupboard which inadvertently had been left open. His mother was horrified and started to scold, but agreed to my suggestion that the three of us had better set to work to clear up the mess, a task into which David entered with gusto. His mother's faith in my methods of dealing with David was particularly taxed when I had to exert authority and David became angry. He would then shout 'shut up, shut up' and stamp his feet. His mother would then hover round looking very anxious wanting, as she told me more than once, to give him a good spanking 'for showing her up'. But she began to realize as time went on that I always remained firm, even though I did not deal with David as she would have done. She was also interested to see that after a scene David and I would re-establish warm and friendly relations through a game with the trains, in which he and I sat on opposite sides of the table so that we could push them across to each other. This game, apart from its probable deeper significance, seemed to give him immediate assurance that our relationship remained intact, despite his outburst of anger. The value of a happy ending to a troubled scene seemed to impress the mother. She also came to see that within a warm relationship David could sometimes be trusted to behave in quite a mature way. This was shown by the regularity with which he returned a key—a much desired object—which I allowed him to play with on this understanding.

A most important part of my work with this child lay in the management of my counter-transference, for this little boy certainly made a great appeal to me from the first moment of contact. His sadness and his unhappy relationship with his mother aroused my compassion. It was essential, therefore, for me to be alert to my positive feelings towards David, as these might easily have led me to succumb to his blandishments. It was also necessary to come to terms with my critical feeling towards the mother which were stimulated by her ineptness in dealing with her child. Within the to and fro of the triangular relationship in which I was involved, there was the possibility that my warmth of feeling for David and his response to me might arouse anxiety and jealousy in the mother who might feel that I was wanting to steal her child. Interpretation of the mother's fears on this score, when it seemed that they were actively present, formed an important part of my work. And from time to time it was necessary to indicate to David that I was aware that he wanted all my interest and attention. For all these reasons I encouraged the mother to share in David's play with me. At first she did so very tentatively, for this was a new experience for her, in fact one of her surprises in our work together was that play with children could be fun. At the end of each session we would all return to the waiting-room so that David could mount the rocking horse, and as he said, ride home to mummy, daddy and Julia. This became a rite which David never allowed me to neglect. Perhaps it brought home to all of us the *raison d'etre* of our work together.

At the end of six and a half months the mother and I discussed the termination of our work, as she was now thinking that she could manage alone. David was duly informed of our decision and, although he expressed some reluctance, he seemed to accept the idea fairly well. When the last day came his farewells were vigorous and prolonged; he ran back several times to say good-bye. As arranged we met again some weeks later, a visit we all enjoyed. The mother came to see me on two further occasions and for a time we kept in touch by letter. As far as I could then judge all seemed to be going quite well.

Although David and his mother were referred by a health visitor, and although I used the maternity and child welfare centre premises, I was in no way linked with it. Nonetheless, the case emphasizes the importance of establishing ties with the maternity and child welfare services, so that young children and their parents can be referred at an early stage of their problems. The benefits of this in terms of prevention need hardly be stressed. I was extremely fortunate, therefore, in meeting David and his mother before their problem had become unmanageable. I was also fortunate in meeting them at a time of crisis when both were in urgent need of a mediator. Hence the importance of waiving all the usual preliminaries—history-taking and the like—so that I could grasp and hold their distress by offering immediate help. It seemed too that the sessions afforded this young and inexperienced mother opportunities for learning something about the needs of toddlers. On several occasions she said that whereas mothers like herself learned much about infant care from maternity and child welfare clinics, they often did not know how to handle children once they began to walk—a comment which suggests that much educational work remains to be done in various directions.

This casework, by 'doing' as well as interpretation provided opportunities for this mother to learn how to deal with her child, first through example and ultimately through sharing in my play with David. It was interesting to notice how she was gradually becoming able to enter into the sessions. This was a process that could not be hurried and I had to wait patiently for it to happen. It had to develop from a growing awareness that the troubles between herself and David did not spring from him alone, and that she too had been at fault. This was not easy for her and during this period she needed my support and encouragement. For although at our first meeting she had asked who was the troublemaker, it was quite clear that at that point, in her view, David was the real offender. Through the medium of play and by observing my handling of David and his responses to me it became possible for this mother to discover the positive aspects of her little son, while he in turn discovered the pleasure of her approval. It will be evident that many of the background problems in the lives of David and his mother were left untouched. For instance, David's relationship with his little sister Julia never came much into the open. He spoke of her from time to time and always with affection. But to what extent she was a source of jealousy I never really knew. On a few occasions the mother brought her to the centre, having no one with whom to leave her. David allowed her to play with the toys, but I saw to it that the session continued as far as possible in the usual way. Although the mother talked to me about the father, he too was not mentioned by David, though after the conclusion of the weekly sessions I saw the mother alone twice as she wanted to discuss some aspects of her married life. But despite the relatively narrow field of our operations it seemed some help was given. For as time went on the mother spoke spontaneously of a lessening of tension between herself and David and improved behaviour on his part; in fact mother and child began to enjoy each other.

7

CHRONIC SORROW: A RESPONSE TO HAVING A MENTALLY DEFECTIVE CHILD*

SIMON OLSHANSKY

THE purpose of this article is twofold: (1) to propose that most parents who have a mentally retarded child suffer from a pervasive psychological reaction, chronic sorrow, that has not always been recognized by the professional personnel—physicians, psychologists, and social workers—who attempt to help them; and (2) to suggest some of the implications of the phenomenon of chronic sorrow for the parent counselling process. This discussion is based on the author's personal and professional experiences and on the experience of the Children's Developmental Clinic staff in counselling parents of severely retarded children.

Most parents who have a mentally defective child suffer chronic sorrow throughout their lives regardless of whether the child is kept at home or is 'put away'. The intensity of this sorrow varies from time to time for the same person, from situation to situation, and from one family to another. The sorrow may be more intense for one parent than for the other in the same family. Many factors, such as a parent's personality, ethnic group, religion, and social class, influence the intensity of this sorrow. Some parents show their sorrow clearly; others attempt to conceal it, and sometimes they succeed. The need to keep a 'stiff upper lip', especially outside the privacy of the home, is a common defence of parents. Anglo-Saxon parents in particular usually feel this need. Although chronic sorrow may be experienced by some parents of minimally retarded children, this reaction is probably more nearly universal among parents whose children are severely or moderately retarded—whose children would be considered retarded in any society and in any cultural group.

The helping professions have somewhat belaboured the tendency

* Published in *Social Casework*, Vol. XLIII, No. 4, April 1962.

of the parent to deny the reality of his child's mental deficiency. Few workers have reported what is probably a more frequent occurrence, the parent's tendency to deny his chronic sorrow. This tendency is often reinforced by the professional helper's habit of viewing chronic sorrow as a neurotic manifestation rather than as a natural and understandable response to a tragic fact. All the parental reactions reported in the literature, such as guilt, shame, and anger, may well be intertwined with chronic sorrow. Moreover, a parent's experiencing chronic sorrow does not preclude his deriving satisfaction and joy from his child's modest achievements in growth and development. It can also be assumed that the child's mental defectiveness has symbolic meaning, on an unconscious level, to some parents. The data that support this assumption, however, are rarely communicated by the parent except in deep psychotherapy.

The reality faced by the parent of a severely retarded child is such as to justify his chronic sorrow. When the parent is asked to 'accept' mental deficiency, it is not clear just what he is being asked to do. The great stress professional workers tend to place on 'acceptance' may suggest to the parent that he is expected to perceive his child from the point of view of the professional helper. This expectation may make him both resentful and resistant. In our clinical experience, we have seen relatively few parents so neurotic that they denied the fact that the child was mentally defective. We have seen relatively few parents who did not recover enough, after the initial shock of discovery, to mobilize their efforts in behalf of the child. It is understandable that some parents move slowly and erratically towards recognition of the mental defect and towards meeting the child's special needs. Some of them even 'regress' to the point of denying, at certain times, the reality of the child's defectiveness. On other occasions they become unduly optimistic about the child's potentialities. In our view, such regression may help the parent to tolerate better the terrible reality that confronts him each day.

Why does the professional worker become so impatient with the parent's slowness or occasional regression and why does he feel such a great sense of urgency to do something about it? After all, the parent has a lifetime in which to learn to deal with the needs and problems of a mentally defective child. In most cases one can ask what will be lost if the parent is unable for several years to view his child as mentally defective. The parents of one of our clinic patients have told us that their child was six or seven years old before they knew definitely that she was mentally defective. Although they had sensed that her development was slow, they had failed to act on their suspicions until her sub normality became self-evident. In what way had the parents been worse off in their 'blissful ignorance'? In what way had the child been worse off, since she had had the capacity to meet the parents' expectations?

The parents of a normal child have to endure many woes, many trials, and many moments of despair. Almost all these parents know, however, that ultimately the child will become a self-sufficient adult. By contrast, the parents of a mentally defective child have little to look forward to; they will always be burdened by the child's unrelenting demands and unbated dependency. The woes, the trials, the moments of despair will continue until either their own deaths or the child's death. Concern about what will happen to his child after he is dead may be a realistic concern for a parent, or it may be associated with death wishes, either for himself or for his child. Release from his chronic sorrow may be obtainable only through death.

What are some of the implications of the parent's chronic sorrow for the professional person who attempts to help him? First, the professional worker should abandon the simplistic and static concept of parental acceptance. Every parent—whether he has a normal or a mentally defective child—accepts his child and rejects his child at various times and in various situations. If both acceptance and rejection are universal parental responses, it is not clear just what the professional person is asking the parent of a mentally defective child to accept. Is the parent being asked to accept the fact that the child is defective? This the parent does, in general. Is he being asked to meet the child's needs realistically? This the parent tries to do, by and large. Is he being asked to abandon his chronic sorrow? This the parent wishes he could do but cannot. The permanent, day-by-day dependence of the child, the interminable frustrations resulting from the child's relative changelessness, the unaesthetic quality of mental defectiveness, the deep symbolism buried in the process of giving birth to a defective child, all these join together to produce the parent's chronic sorrow. That so many parents bear this sorrow stoically is rich testimony to parental courage and endurance. (One might ask, for example, how much progress would have been achieved in the field of rehabilitation if the issue of 'acceptance' had been made the primary focus of professional concern rather than the issue of managing the disability most efficiently through the use of prosthetic devices.)

Second, the professional person's perceptions of the parent will be different if he accepts the idea that chronic sorrow is a natural, rather than a neurotic, reaction. The worker's changed perceptions of the parent and his feelings may encourage the parent to discuss his chronic sorrow more openly and freely. There is a danger that some workers will become over involved and sentimental, so that they will serve as 'wailing walls' rather than as helpers. This danger, however, is always present in any helping situation if a worker surrenders the discipline, restraint and understanding he must have to fulfil his helping role. Although chronic sorrow is a natural, rather than a neurotic, response to a tragic fact, some parents do respond neurotically to their child's handicap and may require treatment for their neurosis. Judging from our experience, however, the number of neurotic parents is small. It is regrettable that this small number of people has received so much professional attention that the tragedy of having a mentally defective child has been viewed less as a tragedy than as a psychiatric problem.

The professional worker who learns to accept chronic sorrow as a normal psychological reaction will grant the parent a longer period of time than otherwise in which to adjust his feelings and organize his resources, both internal and external, to meet the child's needs. The worker will also plan to extend the length of the counselling process. He will alter the usual practice of telling the parent the facts about the child's mental defectiveness in as few as one to four interviews, since the worker will realize that the communication of facts is only one part of the counselling process and is not necessarily the most important part. Some parents may require months, or even years, of counselling before they can muster and maintain the strength and stamina needed to live with the tragedy of having a mentally defective child. What the parent requires, beyond a knowledge of the facts, is an opportunity to ventilate and clarify his feelings and to receive support for the legitimacy of the feelings he is expressing. In some instances the parent will need to be given this opportunity at various times throughout his life.

In addition to providing more time during which the parent can learn to face his problem, and to offering counselling at a slower pace, the worker should also make himself accessible to the parent over a long period of time. No matter how effective the counselling is, many parents need to discuss their feelings and the problems associated with a defective child on many occasions. This need for repeated counselling is natural and should not be considered a sign of either regression or neurosis. The experience of our clinic has demonstrated the importance of accessibility—an 'open door' policy—for the parents of mentally defective children. A parent may telephone a staff member again and again about a recurring problem, a new problem, an emerging crisis, or his own distress.

Finally, if the worker accepts the validity of the concept of chronic sorrow, his goal in counselling the parent will be to increase the parent's comfortableness in living with and managing his defective child. In addition to providing psychological help, the worker will emphasize, more than formerly, the help the mother needs in order to learn to manage such problems as how to feed, discipline, and toilet-train the child. Use of such facilities as pre-school nurseries, special education classes, day care centres, and sheltered workshops should be made available when they can be used appropriately. Moreover, the mother should be given an opportunity to be away from the child at recurring intervals. Although some workers tend to discount the value of 'baby sitting' services, these services can make it possible for the mother to get much-needed relief and can enhance her sense of personal comfort. Greater comfortableness may help make her chronic sorrow more tolerable and may increase her effectiveness in meeting the child's continuing needs. Also, through increased comfortableness the parents may become more accessible to psychological help for themselves.

In summary, it has been suggested that the parent of a mentally defective child suffers from chronic sorrow. This sorrow is a natural response to a tragic fact. If the professional worker accepts chronic sorrow as a natural, rather than a neurotic, response, he can be more effective in helping the parent achieve the goal of increased comfort in living with and managing a mentally defective child.

8

CHILDREN AT RISK*

ELIZABETH E. IRVINE

DR GERALD CAPLAN has familiarized us, in several publications,[1][2][3] with the crisis model of mental health and mental disorder. This draws our attention to certain kinds of sharp discontinuity in development or experience which upset the equilibrium of the individual and expose him to the risk of adopting solutions which are dangerous for his future mental health. Not everyone will emerge from his crisis thus damaged. Some will have responded to the challenge by mobilizing their forces in ways which increase strength and confidence, maturity and ability to cope with stress. Those who emerge weakened, relying more heavily than before on rigid, brittle and maladaptive defences, may well have been predictably more vulnerable at the outset, though Caplan shows reason to believe that the quality of social interaction during the crisis period can often have a decisive effect on the outcome. Young children are particularly vulnerable to separation from their mothers, as Dr John Bowlby and others have demonstrated,[4][5] whereas the mother's reliable presence often renders them surprisingly invulnerable to any stress situation which does not upset the mother herself too greatly. It also seems likely that disturbed relationships within the family, especially but not exclusively between the child and his mother, will enhance his vulnerability to most kinds of stress.

It follows from this reasoning that preventive mental health programmes must be specially concerned to identify and support vulner-

* Published in Case Conference, Vol. X, No. 10, April 1964.
[1] G. Caplan, Concepts of Mental Health and Consultation, U.S. Children's Bureau, 1959.
[2] G. Caplan, A Community Approach to Mental Health, Tavistock Publications, London, 1961.
[3] G. Caplan, Prevention of Mental Disorders in Children, Tavistock Publications, London, 1962.
[4] J. Bowlby, Maternal Care and Mental Health, W.H.O., 1951.
[5] J. Bowlby and M. Ainsworth, 'The Effects of Mother-child Separation: a Follow-Up Study', British Journal of Medical Psychology, Vol. XXIX, Parts 3 and 4, pp. 211-47, 1956.

able individuals who are exposed to crisis situations. One such group, which as yet has received surprisingly little attention, comprises the children of parents who have recently been admitted to a mental hospital. Such children are likely to be particularly vulnerable on account of previous disturbed relationships within the family, especially if the onset of the illness has been insidious, and they are now exposed not only to the sudden loss of a parent, in circumstances which are likely to tinge the natural grief and distress with a heavy colouring of anxiety and guilt. Some of these children may also be vulnerable by heredity. This hypothesis was at one time derived from the tendency of mental illness to run in families, but it now seems likely that much of this tendency could be accounted for by disturbed relationships and the experiences of recurrent crisis.

If this reasoning is correct, policy and practice in the treatment and care of the mentally ill should always take the interests of the children explicitly into account in order to harmonize or balance them with those of the patient. There is as yet little evidence that this is systematically done. A very few hospitals are experimentally admitting pre-school children with their mentally ill mothers.[1][2][3] This is usually advocated on the grounds of benefit to the mother, but it is believed to be of value to the children too, both as avoiding a separation and as affording an opportunity for the child to enjoy skilled support in dealing with the problems with which his mother's illness confronts him. Where no such arrangements exist, the children are automatically separated from the parent who goes into hospital. We should not underestimate the traumatic potential of separation from the father, which will vary according to the age of the child and the degree of attachment to him. Separation from the mother, however, often results in substitute care arrangements which involve separation from the father also, whereas if the father goes to hospital the children are likely to remain with their mother. Such arrangements may be formal and official, in which case the child care service takes responsibility and is in a position to help the child deal with his inner crisis; or they may be unofficial, as when relatives open their homes to one or more children. In this case it is nobody's explicit job to make sure that the child is dealing adequately with the crisis, and the lack of public discussion suggests that social workers may be too busy dealing with

[1] G. Douglas, 'Psychotic Mothers', *The Lancet*, 1956, pp. 124, 125.
[2] A. A. Baker, J. A. Game, M. Morrison and J. G. Thorpe, 'Admitting Schizophrenic Mothers with their Babies', *The Lancet*, II, 1961, pp. 237-9.
[3] T. Goser, 'A Unit for Mother and Babies in a Psychiatric Hospital', *Journal of Child Psychology and Psychiatry*, Vol. III, No. 1, 1962.

other urgent problems to investigate whether the relatives are indeed able to give the child the help he needs.

How far can we assume that placement in a kindly family, related or otherwise, provides an adequate solution for the child's emotional needs? Even in the simpler case where the mother goes to hospital for physical illness, this is expecting a lot. Adults often find it difficult to tolerate a child's grief or his defences, or to let him express his feelings. If he is sad and listless, unable to respond affectionately, and particularly if he eats poorly and compares the food unfavourably with his mother's cooking, those who are trying so hard to make him happy often feel hurt and personally rejected. This is likely to be all the more so if the mother is insane, and if her behaviour and care of the children has been a subject of dissatisfaction and friction for some time, or if there were other tensions between her and the relatives now caring for the children. Other adults can readily sympathize with the child who grieves openly, but may be shocked or antagonized by one who wears a mask of indifference, is unnaturally cheerful, or who expresses hostility to the absent parent. These reactions may be taken at their face value, and the child perceived as a heartless little wretch, whereas a child who is using these defences is probably in need of professional understanding and help. Yet other children may express their emotional disturbance by rudeness and rebellion towards anyone who presumes to try to replace the absent parent, or develop symptoms such as tics, enuresis or soiling. Many adults find it hard to recognize such behaviour as a signal of distress, and their sympathy may be alienated. There is another hazard when the absent parent is mentally ill; these manifestations are apt to be interpreted as the first signs of hereditary mental illness, in which case the child will be treated with anxious over-solicitude, or those in charge may try to protect themselves against this anxiety by nagging or scolding him in the hope that he will stop it, and so prove that he is not ill after all.

When a parent goes to hospital, the mere fact of separation, the pain of missing the absent person, is bound to be complicated more or less by anxiety about the illness and the outcome, and by guilt for past unkindness, demandingness or thoughtlessness. Where these feelings are strong the child will need opportunity to talk them out; this some families or foster-parents can provide, but others may find it too hard to tolerate the expression of such feelings, and may smother it with reassurance or cheerful chatter in a way that relieves themselves more than the child. When the parent is mentally ill, everyone's anxieties are likely to be worse. Physical illness can often be labelled and explained, and the length of absence can often be predicted; this is helpful to all but the youngest children. Mental illness can usually not be named or explained, and questions are apt to evoke uneasy equivocation, which creates an atmosphere of shameful and embarrassing mystery. Older children may suspect madness, and will feel ashamed of this as they would not of a physical complaint. Guilt may well have been stimulated during the period of onset by repeated urging to be good, to keep quiet, for fear of giving mother a headache, because daddy isn't well. They may have been more overtly accused of 'getting on mother's nerves', or of 'driving daddy round the bend'. When their mother or father eventually 'goes round the bend' this will seem to be the fulfilment of a prophecy, the result of all those unheeded warnings. There may have been scenes of violence, and the children may have not only been very frightened, but also quite confused about who was the victim and who the aggressor. This is especially so if the child has been attached to a paranoid parent, who may for months or years have been accusing neighbours, relatives or other parent of conspiring to 'put him (her) away'. Now he has been 'put away', so he was right all along; or perhaps the child feels that he has been sent away as a punishment for difficult behaviour. Such children are apt to be both frightened and angry with those who 'put away' the missing parent for obscure reasons which they are usually too embarrassed to explain. The children therefore 'play up' in ways which set up a new round of anger and anxiety in relatives, since they seem to confirm all the natural fears about heredity.

For all these reasons, the children of parents who have recently entered a mental hospital need help which relatives, friends or foster-parents *may* be able to give, but on the other hand may not, on account of their own anxieties about grief and loss, and about mental illness in particular. Moreover, they need this help *now*. Within a few weeks they will have resolved the crisis one way or the other. If they adopt pathological defences and we wait until these have become so crippling or alarming that they eventually get referred for treatment, it may well take years to undo what could have been prevented by a few timely interviews with the child or the adults about him. This is why an adequate preventive mental health programme would require that in every case where the patient has children someone should take responsibility, not only for seeing that they are being suitably cared for on the material level, but also that they are being allowed or helped to express their feelings freely, and to overcome unrealistic anxiety and guilt—which are not susceptible to reassurance unless they have been fully expressed to someone who does not secretly or openly share them. Sometimes, as I mentioned in a former paper,[1] a parent or other member of the household may in fact be blaming the child as a way of dealing with his own intolerable guilt, and this may require more extensive casework help.

Even where the separation crisis has been dealt with, further crises may arise from the patient's visits home. Moods may vary alarmingly, disappointments may lead to threats of breaking up the home and sending the children away. If the children are in care, there may be jealousy and rows with the foster-parents. At all these points help may be needed. The parent's return home will necessitate further re-adjustments, especially when he or she is still far from well. Fortunately simple supportive casework, not too time-consuming in kind, can often prove remarkably effective. Mrs A, the mother of several children, returned home against advice after a long stay in a mental hospital, following a limited response to one of the new drugs. Her eldest son, who had been living alone with father meanwhile (the younger children being in care) committed a minor offence soon after his mother's return, and was put on probation. Mrs A, who was still quite vague and confused, began to demand the return of the other children too, and there were grounds for concern about all these children if she got her way. However, with the support of the proba-tion officer the mother gradually improved, the younger children came home and settled down, and the eldest boy did not repeat his offence. As the probation officer eventually expressed it: 'I think what helped him most was to know that I liked his mother and was not frightened by her in spite of her strangeness'.

Not all children are so lucky, especially those with a parent who spends short periods in a mental hospital at frequent intervals. Health visitors are sometimes concerned about young children in this situa-tion, as with Mrs B, whose husband sent her back to hospital when-ever her appetite failed, but took her home again as soon as it recovered, even though she was still in terror of enemies whom she felt to be pursuing her with machine-guns from aeroplanes, and talked about this in a loud and agitated manner to the children and everyone else who would listen. These children were observed to be very strained and withdrawn whenever their mother was at home, and more happy and spontaneous when she was away. The health visitor arranged for her little boy (aged twenty months) to enter a day

[1] E. E. Irvine, 'Psychosis in Parents: Mental Illness as a Problem for the Family', *British Journal of Psychiatric Social Work*, Vol. VI, No. 1, Spring 1961

nursery, where for some time he was exceptionally difficult and with-drawn. He gradually improved, but was visibly disturbed at each recurrent separation and reunion with his mother. Eventually he became able to enjoy the opportunities for play in the nursery and respond to the staff, though still a solitary child at four years. The warm and stable environment provided by the nursery was probably an important factor in this child's gradual improvement.

In a recent symposium entitled *Reluctantly to School*[1] two authors[2][3] stress the frequency of ambulant mental illness in the parents of school refusers, particularly in the mothers. Walker[2] describes two examples, of which I shall summarize one. An unmarried mother was epileptic and was periodically admitted to hospital for severe depression. Her mother looked after the three children at these times but died when the eldest boy was ten. From this time he felt increasingly responsible for his mother and siblings, especially for reminding his mother to take her medicine, and school attendance suffered. At twelve he was brought before a juvenile court for non-attendance, and following an adjournment in custody he was enabled to return to school with the help of the probation officer and the mental welfare officer, who was now presumably called in to relieve the boy of the home nursing which he had been doing unaided for two years.

This story illustrates how easily cases can slip through the after-care net, even when the family is in no state to undertake responsibility for the patient, and may be in urgent need of supportive and preventive services itself. It is unclear at the moment how far this is due to the undermanning of services, and how far to lack of liaison between mental hospitals and community services, whether specialized or not. The problem is too big to be solved by specialized services alone, even when the mental hospital really brings itself to trust and use the com-munity services. Child care officers, probation officers and health visitors all have contact with these families, and the help they offer can be tremendously increased by communication and co-operation with those treating the parent. It is vital that there should be some machinery for ensuring that *somebody* is available and sensitive to the needs of every family exposed to such stress, or at least every family containing children, so that no family in need slips through the net unhelped. We do not know what proportion of these families can manage unaided— not simply to survive intact, but in such a way as to avoid developing

[1] *British Journal of Psychiatric Social Work*, Vol. VII, No. 2, Autumn, 1963.
[2] A. Walker, 'Children who Refuse to go to School in a Reception Centre', ibid.
[3] E. Burgess, 'Children Committed to Care for Non-attendance at School', ibid.

G

a fresh round of mental disturbance. We do know that at present many are left to manage as best they can. We need a study of how families cope with this crisis similar to that reported by Caplan[1], of families coping with the birth of a premature baby. The other necessity is that all professional people who have contact with such families should be recognized as potential helpers, and that those who do not already have adequate or appropriate training should recognize the need for consultation, and should be generously supported by those with more specialized knowledge, whether of mental illness, or of casework method.

[1] *A Community Approach to Mental Health*, op. cit.

9

HELPING A CHILD ADAPT TO STRESS: THE USE OF EGO PSYCHOLOGY IN CASEWORK*

A. KATHARINE LLOYD

THE Freudian concept of the id, the ego, and the superego has become part of our thinking in diagnostic casework, but the recent emphasis on the role of the ego in the functioning of the total personality is of particular interest to caseworkers. We are realizing more and more that it is not enough to understand unconscious drives and motivations but that we must be aware also of the ego's cognitive, selective, and synthesizing powers, as these are even more important for the maintenance of personality structure and for creating the conditions for healthy and creative living.

The good ego is able to perceive both inner drives and outer reality pressures and preserve an equilibrium between the two. It can select that which is important from that which is trivial. It is able to meet first things first, to concentrate on one thing at a time. It can synthesize so that the whole personality, stresses and strains notwithstanding, functions smoothly and harmoniously. The person with a good ego has, like a humming top, a 'still centre' within himself which is part of his whole movement, is in touch with every part, and is notwithstanding always at rest.[1] This is the 'I' part of the personality, the self-awareness that is the centre of consciousness and is able to relate to other consciousness, to the 'I' in other people. At first this consciousness is turned in on itself. The small child who says for the first time, 'I want to do it all by myself—I did do it all by myself, didn't I?' has reached an important stage in his growing. But he is still admiring himself. If he reaches maturity, he will ultimately be able as John

---

* Published in *The Social Service Review*, Vol. XXXI, No. 1, March 1957.
[1] This simile comes from Dorothy Sayers' novel, *Gaudy Night*, Victor Gollancz, London, 1935, pp. 170-1

Macmurray says, to live more and more 'in terms of the object'.[1] Out of his sense of being loved and accepted and admired for what he can do, he can reach out and become aware of the needs and sensitivities of others. Moreover, it is in the 'I' or, as usually termed, the 'ego' that the 'I want' of the id and the 'I ought' of the superego come to terms with one another. When the ego is weak, there may be such strife and turmoil between the surge of impulse from the id and the harsh punitive response of the superego that the person is overwhelmed and locked in conflict, unable to perceive, to synthesize, or to control. But when the ego is strong and steady, the tension does not overwhelm but is brought under control and translated into purposeful and perhaps creative action.

In this article it is proposed to study the case of a child whose ego development has suffered probably as a result of trauma in her early life-experience. She is confronted with a problem too big for her to perceive and grasp, and she is assisted in her attempts to understand and solve it by the skill of a social worker well versed in methods of supportive treatment. The treatment is, in fact, a demonstration of the application of the principles of ego psychology in casework.

An eight-year-old girl, Sue Archer, is admitted to a large urban hospital for repair surgery on her cleft lip and palate. She is referred to the social service department by an agency that had known of the girl through preliminary medical evaluation in her home town where there were no facilities for this type of surgery. In the past there had been difficulty at the time of hospitalization in helping Sue to separate from her mother and to co-operate with medical personnel.

The family, consisting of Sue, the parents, and two younger children, lives in a small town. Mr Archer has a small but steady income on which the family seems to manage adequately. The atmosphere in the home was described by the referring agency as comfortable and accepting, and family relationships were said to be good. Mrs Archer had, however, become extremely upset at the sight of Sue after birth because the child's face was so malformed. There appeared to have been some initial rejection, and the mother now admits that she and Mr Archer are more protective of Sue than of the other girls because of her deformity. At four months of age, Sue was admitted to a hospital for repair surgery, but she cried so much that much of the work broke down. Again at the age of six and a half she was admitted for additional surgery, which was only somewhat more successful. At present she has a short, tight upper lip, an enlarged nose opening on one side, and

[1] *Reason and Emotion*, Faber & Faber, London, 1935, p. 32.

an asymmetry of the face because one eye is pulled slightly lower than the other. Her speech is defective because of palate malformation. This has kept her out of school. She is very conscious of her appearance and talks of wanting to be pretty. When the parents visited some days after Sue's admission, the worker noted that they were both warm and affectionate with Sue and that they were unsophisticated, unassuming people, interested in co-operating in any medical planning.

This quotation from the record gives a succint description of the problem. This child had to face an ordeal of surgery which would be a severe one even for an adult. If the third operation which she is now to undergo is to be successful, she will have to co-operate with the surgeon to the extent of enduring having her jaw wired immobile for six weeks. During this time she will have to be fed through a tube. In order to help the hospital decide on the best way to care for Sue, one consultation was requested with the psychiatrist. The psychiatrist considered Sue a well-integrated child whose main problem was trauma in relation to surgery. She recommended that Sue should have supportive help from the social worker so that she could express and work through her fears about the operation. The psychiatrist also recommended that the social worker talk with the child about the details of the operation so that she might know specifically what to expect before, during, and after surgery.

The social worker can discern from the history something of this child's motivation and capacity for understanding and facing her problem. Sue is conscious of her appearance and concerned about it, and she wants to be different—to look pretty and to speak properly. This improved appearance cannot be obtained, however, unless she is able to undergo a painful surgical ordeal and to spend many weeks away from her home. She must forgo the comfort of the moment in order to obtain gratification in the future. She knows what she wants, but, as Dr French has pointed out, 'to be of any use at all efforts to achieve a goal must be guided by practical understanding of the problem to be solved, by some kind of plan for achieving one's purpose'.[1] The mature adult is expected to have a well-developed sense of time and place. He can understand that an ordeal will not last long, that next week or next month will inevitably arrive. He can keep the image of his family and his home alive in his mind. The child cannot do this. A very young child has little sense of time and little ability to wait. Even a four-year-old cannot look ahead more than a few days. An

[1] Thomas M. French, M.D., *The Integration of Behavior*, Vol. I: *Basic Postulates*, University of Chicago Press, Chicago, 1952, p. 53.

eight-year-old has more comprehension of time and place, but here too, we see one of the moist poignant contrasts between youth and age. For the child one spring is a lifetime; for the adult it is here and gone in a flash, hardly perceived before it is over. This factor of time perception in the young ego has great importance for the child facing a problem of hospitalization, a child who may become overwhelmed with present frustration and quite unable to grasp the fact that this ordeal will help toward attaining the longed-for goal.

Although this is not her only problem, Sue does find it hard to look ahead. In her impatience she tends to regress and cry and resist like a much younger child. If she is to solve this problem she will need to enlarge her adaptive and her integrative capacities—both essentially functions of the ego. As Alexander puts it: 'Before the integrative functions of the ego have developed, every impulse seeks gratification without regard to the needs of the total organism. If angered, the child will show temper by kicking, screaming, and indiscriminately hostile behaviour. . . . The reality principle means carefully planned and co-ordinated behaviour which often requires voluntarily imposed restrictions and effort but ensures more gratification.'[1] For this child, much depends on the intensity of the hope within her, as this will affect the degree of her motivation. Here she can be greatly helped by constructive identification, perhaps the chief means by which the ego grows and develops. She can understand that her parents want this for her and can join her hope to theirs. In addition—and this is very important —while she is in the hospital the caseworker becomes an additional mother figure who also has this hope for her. The worker is even more than this: she becomes a kind of resource person who can be used alternately as someone with whom the child has a positive identification and as someone on whom she can within limits release her anger and her frustration. The relationship with the social worker will be the means of holding and enhancing the child's motivation to improve her appearance, as well as of helping her to learn what the ordeal ahead will be and to work out her feelings about it. Much depends upon Sue's capacity to form a good relationship with the worker. There are signs in the history that Sue has this capacity; e.g. she has a good family background, good relationships with parents, and good intelligence, and it soon becomes apparent that she can relate well and make a good adjustment on the ward. To this extent her capacity is good.

[1] Franz Alexander, M.D., *Fundamentals of Psychoanalysis*, W. W. Norton & Co., New York, 1948, p. 90.

There are, however, other factors that complicate the problem. This child becomes extremely frightened in hospital situations because she is unable to look past the trauma of the moment to the hope of the future. Why is her ego so weak in perception and in the capacity for self-control? Some eight-year-old children can sustain painful experiences with little apparent strain. But with Sue it seems possible that her low tolerance for traumatic experiences— even comparatively minor ones such as dental treatment—stems from her early nurture.

It has been suggested that 'at the beginning of life, the infantile organism is governed by the vital body needs for respiration, sleep, intake of food, evacuation, skin comfort and movement, which are the forerunners and first representatives of the basic drives. They impinge on the mind with the sensations of tension and relief which arise in connection with them. . . . The rudiments of the ego, as they emerge gradually in the first half of the first year of life, take their pattern from the environmental conditions which have left their imprint on the infant's mind by way of his early pleasure-pain experiences, the conditions themselves becoming internalized in the ego structure. . . . Whenever the smooth sequence of need-tension-relief is upset and the mental representative of a need or drive is weighed down by memory of intense unpleasure connected with it, the door is open for the same area or function to be used later for the playing out of neurotic conflicts.'[1] As the most important of all these early experiences is the feeding experience, much depends on the baby's capacity to suck and on the tenderness and loving care of the mother, who inevitably communicates her feeling as she holds him and feeds him. A child who cannot suck at all may die. One whose sucking powers are impaired through deformity of the mouth is unlikely to have the same satisfactory experience as the normal child. Moreover, it is unlikely that a mother and a child with a deformity of the mouth can have quite the same joy in one another's company. The normal baby's mother can relate to him without undue strain. The deformed baby's mother, on the other hand, may be either horrified and withdrawn or may develop a reaction formation of becoming overpitiful and overprotective. Either way it will be difficult for her to be spontaneous and free in her feeling.

In the Archer case we are told that family relationships are good. This would seem to be confirmed by the considerable strengths that Sue possesses in spite of her deformity. The fact that Sue's sense of

[1] Anna Freud, 'Psychoanalysis and Education', Psychoanalytic Study of the Child, IX, 11-12, 13, 14, 1954.

security is slight may be partly accounted for by deficiencies in the early feeding experience. At four months this child was hospitalized and presumably separated from her mother. It was not only the surgery that broke down at this time but possibly also something of the baby's developing trust in her environment. As Erikson suggests, it is in the oral stage that the baby first learns to trust. It is in these early months that he discovers that living can be a warm, friendly, comfortable process in which he can suck to repletion and be soothed to sleep. Erikson says that 'the infant's first social achievement . . . is his willingness to let the mother out of sight without undue anxiety or rage, because she has become an inner certainty as well as an outer predictability.'[1] Certainly Sue's early experiences may have done something to her sense of security that made her fearful and caused her to be at the mercy of instinctual anxieties which welled up in later years in times of stress. These anxieties overwhelm her motivation to be brave and to face the operation that is to 'make her pretty'. Thus, she comes into the hospital certainly as an ambivalently loved child without the firm foundation of trust in her environment which might have been hers had the first months been less traumatic. Moreover, she probably dreads the reactions of other children. She is fearful, and her ego is impoverished by her fear and self-consciousness caused by her deformity. It will be hard for her to tolerate separation from her family and worse still to allow the doctors to operate on her mouth, which has already been the source of so much frustration and pain. She does not understand her unconscious fears about letting people touch her mouth, nor would it be possible or advisable for her to understand them at this stage of her development. She must be helped to face the reality problem of the operation in other ways. Here lies the challenge to the social worker as she thinks out a plan of treatment. The worker has to establish a relationship with the child and then within the security of that relationship help her first to adjust to a new environment and then learn step by step what she must face within it. It will be most important to partialize the experience so that the child does not need to cope with too much at a time. At the same time, as she learns, she will need to have an opportunity to work out her feelings about this painful learning.

At first Sue is very defensive. The worker's task is to help her to move to the use of more constructive defences than those of denial, escape, regression, and projection. In the beginning Sue alternately

[1] Erik H. Erikson, *Childhood and Society*, W. W. Norton & Co., New York, 1950, p. 219.

tries to escape from the painful situation or to fight it or project responsibility for it on her doctors, saying that they want to hurt her. As she becomes more secure with the worker, however, she is able temporarily to lay aside these defences and discuss the problem with the worker a little at a time. She more and more identifies positively with the worker. She also gets great help by means of playing out an identification with the doctor who appears to her as an aggressor. In this role she works out her feelings by pretending to attack the social worker. This helps her to gain a sense of mastery of the situation. At the end of the three weeks she really has made some progress in coming to grips with the reality of a painful situation, and she is able to verbalize her desire to have the operation. The doubtful factor throughout is the strength of her instinctual feelings of anxiety which cause her to vomit when pressed too far. Perhaps it is this factor which finally made the surgeon decide to postpone the operation until Sue is older.

Let us now go stage by stage through the supportive work done with this child and see how the worker's skill deals with solving the problem—or moves toward solving it.

Stage I: Adjustment to the Hospital Environment

Hospitalization is a frightening experience for any child, especially for a child like Sue who is self-conscious about her appearance, finds talking difficult, and can read and write very little. Accordingly, there is a recommendation from the psychiatrist that the child receive as much individual attention as possible. Head nurse and resident are to take a special interest in her and the social worker is to visit each day. This child's roots are in her happy home life, and the reality for her is home—mother, father, sisters, and the things they do together. The worker on her first visit begins where the child is.

When I first visited Sue she was sitting on her bed in the corner of the ward with her eyes wide open and a blank expression on her face. She is a rather pale child with pretty, light blonde shoulder-length hair, but the asymmetry of her face makes her look very unattractive. I told her my name and that I was a social worker and would be visiting her often. Her initial reaction to me, as it had been to the rest of the staff, was one of very slow acceptance. I said I knew Sue had talked with a lady yesterday (the psychiatrist), who had told me that she wanted to write home. I had brought some picture post cards. If she wanted to write and would like me to help her, I would write for her. She brightened when I said this. This was the first time she smiled at me. She began musing aloud as to what various family members were doing. She asked me to write the first card to her mother to see if her work was finished. I asked why she asked this, and she replied it was because her mother had promised she would visit when her work was done. This anxiety about visiting was not expressed in the card to her father, but rather a feeling of friendly interest in what he was doing. She told me what her sisters were probably doing and guessed they both missed her. I said she was probably missing all of them a little, too, but we liked her here, and she would soon get to know us real well and would have fun here. We talked about the things she liked to do, and when I left she asked that I return the next day.

In all this the worker is recognizing what home means to the child— talking with her about the loved people and what they are doing and sending them picture post cards as the child directs. In this way she keeps the reality of home alive in the child's mind. Much later in their contact, the need of doing this often is demonstrated when she finds Sue rather unhappy on a Saturday.

When I reminded her that I would be unable to visit her the next day she grabbed the keys from my pocket, saying, 'I'll lock you in jail and see how you feel'. After I recognized her impatience with being in the hospital so long and accepted her feelings about it, she told me to read to her. While she ate lunch I read from *The Wizard of Oz*. She expressed feeling about not wanting to get lost as Dorothy had in the story. She did not answer when I asked if she felt lost. I went over in detail exactly where she was, pointing out that she couldn't be lost as her mother and father and all of us knew exactly where she was. As I left she voluntarily handed me my keys and appeared content.

It is only after talking about home that the worker moves on to building up in the child a sense of being liked and accepted in the hospital. She moves slowly in building up the relationship and does not hurry the child into learning what she must do in connection with the problem of the operation. Meantime, the worker is busy also in assessing the child's strengths and the level on which she can relate.

In visits during Sue's first few days in the hospital, our time was spent in having fun and doing things together so that we could get to know one another. Among other things, we played with paper dolls and talked about them. She also talked about her younger sister, who was the pretty one of the family, and brought out some indirect expression of feeling about her. Her acceptance of me was cautious but progressive and rather intense. I soon found that this slender blonde child had a great deal of appeal and good ability to relate. Eventually, a good relationship was achieved. After her initial shyness was overcome, Sue made a good adjustment on the ward and was well liked by the staff and children.

Sue begins to realize the worker is someone who understands what it is like to be lonely and who helps her to enjoy playing simple games and doing things within her capacity so that even in this strange place she can get some sense of achievement. She comes to understand that this person is a source of strength, a person who does not regard the frightening future as something that cannot be understood and faced. Moreover, apparently this person is going to be there constantly throughout all these new and alarming experiences.

Stage II: Learning to Tolerate Frustration

It was soon learned that orthodontic work would be needed before the operation, and I discussed with the surgeon exactly what was necessary. I learned that the work would consist of applying bands to the teeth so that the jaw could be wired immobile. Sue's tolerance for the surgery which would close her mouth for approximately six weeks could thereby be tested. Sue's first trip to the orthodontia clinic had already been completed before I knew of the plan. It was described as 'a very stormy session', and the psychiatrist recommended that the social worker accompany Sue to the clinic in the future. When I saw Sue I told her that I knew she had been upset by the work done on her teeth a few days ago and that from then on I would meet her in the clinic and stay with her. She brightened and asked that I bring her something for her hair; when I gave her the barrette in clinic next day, she clutched it without smile or comment.

To have one's jaw wired immobile for six weeks would be a difficult experience for anyone. For a child who does not fully comprehend the reason for it or for the tiresome stages leading up to it, it can be, as in Sue's case, an intolerable ordeal. Even the preliminary operation of applying bands to the teeth is frightening for this child, probably because of the painful associations she already has in relation to her mouth. The worker's plan of helping Sue is hindered a little at this stage because, owing to poor administrative planning, the child is taken to the clinic for the first visit without her. Instinctual terror is an overwhelming thing in a child. It is beyond the reach of ordinary reassurance and consolation because temporarily the ego function which perceives and maintains equilibrium between inner and outer stress is overthrown. The surge of inner anxiety, much of it unconscious, wells up in the child, and the ego strength which should enable her to say to herself, 'I know this will not last long; I will sit still,' is not there. The child knows only that she feels frightened and hurt and attacked. She sees the doctor as attacking her as well as hurting her, and so the defence of projection comes into play. It is as if she says to herself, 'I am not crying and resisting because I am naughty and frightened but because someone is attacking me.' This kind of situation is not helped by ordinary reassurance because at this stage the child is beyond the reach of reason. Nothing could be accomplished by deep exploration of the child's disturbed feelings, but a beginning can be made by matter-of-fact recognition of the fact that she feels upset and that the worker understands this. The worker is in fact beginning here to help Sue learn about this new experience, and she tries to make it more tolerable by her presence and her gift to enhance the child's good feature. The worker also interpreted the situation to the orthodontist, who had an important role to play in helping the child.

Dr M, the orthodontist, spent a great deal of time with Sue, always showing interest in her and the 'surprises' (either something I had given her or something she brought from the hospital) which she always had with her. She joked a lot with him and loved to make him laugh. During this visit four bands which Sue called 'bracelets' were fitted to the upper molars, but she would not let the doctor touch her four front lower teeth, which were the only straight teeth in her mouth. I asked why she didn't want the bands on those teeth, and she answered tearfully, 'They are not rotten.' I agreed that they were nice straight teeth and said that the doctor was not going to harm them in any way. The doctor also gave this reassurance, but because Sue was becoming irritable no further work was done that day.

Here the worker is trying to help the child deal with the reality problem of the operation piece by piece. She agrees with the surgeon that this preliminary experience is a good way of helping the child to partialize the problem of the operation. If Sue can learn to endure the work on her teeth, this will be a kind of dress rehearsal for the operation itself.

One of the important factors in ego development is the child's pride in its own body. This child has had little opportunity for pride, but she clings pathetically to what she has.

Stage III: Mastering Feelings about the Problem

The day following our first visit to orthodontia together was the first time Sue began bringing out her feelings directly to me. As we played a game I commented that she had become upset yesterday and that I was very sorry. I would like to help her feel better, and if she wanted to talk to me about it she could. After much laughing and running around the ward, Sue ran up to me, saying, 'I'll cut off your head.' Suddenly she added, 'Let's exchange noses and mouths.' When I agreed to do this her expression, which had become more serious, was mixed with surprise and anticipation. With gestures our features were exchanged, and I then asked, 'How am I now?' Standing motionless and staring into space, she said, 'You're a harelip.' I asked, 'How do I feel being a harelip?' She leaned her elbows on the bed, placed her chin in her hands, and with a sudden surge of feeling said, 'You feel awful.' Then she reverted to her provocative, giggly behaviour, saying my eyes were dirty and that she wanted to operate on them. While she pretended to operate, I said that I had gone to a doctor because my eyes needed fixing and he gave me glasses. It's kind of like her coming here to have the doctor fix her mouth so that she will look better. She feels bad with it this way, and we all want to help her look and feel better. Dr M wants to help, too, and his part is to put bands on her teeth. That has to be done before the operation, so Dr K (the surgeon) can be sure she will be able to hold her mouth still while he operates. She asked if her mouth would be closed, and I asked her to tell me what Dr K had told her. She then showed me how her teeth would be held together and how her lip would be closed. We then talked about what she had just told me. I recognized her anger at Dr M the previous day and gave assurance that it was understandable and that she could talk about it. This was the beginning of Sue's pattern of getting angry in the orthodontic clinic, talking about it with me later, and then taking the step forward to plan how much she would let Dr M do the next time.

This interview shows real movement. Sue is now secure enough in the relationship with the worker to use her as a means of expressing her feelings. At first, she turns her back on the reality that she knows has to be faced. The worker does not push her, but lets her go at her own pace. The child herself expresses her anger, saying, as children so often do when they are angry with someone, 'I'll cut off your head.' Sue is able to move on from this to acting out her feelings about her disfigurement. She feels so closely identified with the worker that she can play out an exchange of feelings with her and use her to bring out her own sense of anger and desperation at being a 'harelip'. Having done that, she moves on to identify herself with the doctor as aggressor; she becomes the hurting and powerful person and pretends to operate on the worker. This defence is very common in children.

Anna Freud regards it as 'one of the most natural and widespread modes of behaviour on the part of the primitive ego'. She points out that 'there are many children's games in which through the metamorphosis of the subject into a dreaded object anxiety is converted into pleasurable security'.[1] While the child is playing out this identification, the worker is able to do some real interpretation and in particular to relate to Sue's basic motivation, that of having her mouth fixed so that she will feel and look better. Once the child has expressed her feelings in this way she is able as she has not been before to enter into serious discussion about the details of the operation. Thus an important stage in learning is reached. Within the relationship the child has expressed her feelings, used her defences more constructively, and so become able to talk realistically about her problem. She has begun to face her fears and is able to understand them a little and to plan for the next ordeal. Her ego has apparently been strengthened in its capacity to perceive the meaning of this traumatic experience and to some extent in its capacity to control the instinctual anxiety which arises out of it.

In the next interview, Sue once more identifies with the aggressor as a means of working out her feelings, but this time Sue co-operates with the worker instead of acting out against her.

On my next visit with Sue I took a doctor's play kit. She examined the equipment and made careful preparation for an operation on a large panda which had acquired a slightly crooked nose. She announced, 'We will operate on her crooked nose'. The stethoscope was placed to the panda's heart, and Sue solemnly said, 'Her heart is fluttering'. I said the panda was scared of the operation, and she answered, 'Yes, and she cries at night'. I was sorry that she felt so frightened and said I would like to help her so she wouldn't be afraid. We listened to the heart and I said it had stopped fluttering and was all right because Panda knew Sue would take good care of her. With much giggling she then ordered me to carry Panda to the bed and hold her. Sue then went to the other end of the room to play with one of the children. However, she kept an eye on me and watched to see that I was taking good care of Panda. After a few minutes, I said Panda was feeling very good after her operation, and I asked if I could leave. Sue said, 'Yes, Panda is all right now'. I told Sue that she would be all right, too, I knew that she was very upset about the operation, but I would be with her as much of the time as possible, and we would all take special care of her. Happily she was content to have me leave then.

[1] *The Ego and the Mechanisms of Defense*, trans. Cecil Baines, International Universities Press, New York, 1946, p. 119.

Sue now becomes identified with the worker and the nurses and others who will look after her. In setting the stage for the game and helping the child to use this defence to the utmost, the worker is giving valid reassurance. She recognizes the child's fears and does not minimize them but she says that she would like to help Sue and that everyone will take good care of her. This play marked a big step forward, although on the next two days Sue reverts to her former defence of denying and escaping from the problem.

A day later, I attempted to talk with Sue about her previous trip to orthodontia and to prepare her for the next visit. Her only comment was that she had not liked it. Then she started running around the ward, laughing and making clownish faces. This kept up for several minutes, so that after several attempts to talk with her I finally told her I must leave for that day. I knew she wanted to talk with me about the work on her teeth, but I couldn't chase her around the room to talk. I promised to be back next day. She accepted this in the same clownish way and was busy making the children laugh at her antics when I left.

The next day, I said that Sue's last visit to the orthodontist hadn't been very pleasant for her, and I would like to help her make the next visit better. While we played with her doll, I brought up the fact that she had become more upset than usual, and I thought it had something to do with her nice lower teeth. At this she turned her back, saying that she would vomit if I talked any more about it. I said I didn't want to upset her, and if she felt that way about it we didn't have to talk today. By the following day Sue brought up the subject herself by indicating that Dr M could work on any of her teeth but the front ones.

I talked with the psychiatrist, who pointed out that Sue's reaction of threatening to vomit if I talked with her further about the orthodontic work was indicative of the way she will react if pushed too fast in the orthodontic work. This is a clue to the importance of recognizing her low rate of tolerance and of going along at her rate of adjustment.

Stage IV: Coming to Grips with the Problem

The worker does all she can to promote co-operation among the different people who are working with this child. After the 'Panda' interview with Sue, the worker talked with the various members of the hospital staff about plans for the child. She reports as follows:

About this time Sue became impatient for surgery and expressed a desire to have it as soon as possible, but in spite of this her tolerance for the orthodontic work remained low.

There are signs of movement here. It seems as if the child is coming to grips with the problem of facing the operation. A very difficult session in the orthodontic clinic follows, however, when the doctor forces Sue to sit still while he cements bands to her lower front teeth; after this Sue manages to express her anger with the doctor quite openly to the worker. She explains how she had felt and how she would bite the doctor's finger if he ever did it again. Then she again plays out her fears by pretending that she is now the doctor and the worker the little girl. She acts out her feelings against the worker, pretending to give her an injection and to work on her eyes and teeth. The worker has to prevent the child from actually poking her in the eye.

She pretended to work on my teeth, and after holding me down said, 'Now vomit'. I said I knew she had vomited in clinic yesterday; that Dr M had forced her to sit still and had made her pretty mad.

After playing all this out, Sue is able to enter into serious discussion, which this time goes further than it ever has before. She does not this time revert to giggly behaviour.

For the first time, Sue entered into a serious discussion about the operation and wondered specifically if she would be fed through a tube. I told her she would and talked with her about the details of the operation and showed how the tube would be inserted at the corner opening of the mouth. Then she played like Dr M 'after the operation' and pretended to take bands off my teeth.

I showed her what loud sounds one could make in the throat and nose, and she was delighted with the results of her own efforts to make the sounds. Very seriously she said perhaps no one would hear her after her mouth was closed. We again practised making loud sounds, and I promised to bring her a bell. I also pointed out that all of us here know she will need extra care after the operation and we will take good care of her. She led me to the door of a room where a child was being fed by stomach tube. Sue expressed a serious interest in the procedure. We talked about it and also talked to the child, who was very friendly. Sue seemed more curious than frightened.

In all this the worker is helping Sue to feel that she can control the situation and not that it will completely control her. She is trying to strengthen the controlling or the executive part of the ego—what we might term in ordinary language 'will power'. It is much easier for the child to control her feelings and to keep still if she knows there are things she can do to control her surroundings, even if they are only small things like ringing a bell. Moreover, it is important that the child herself takes the initiative in finding out about the process of tube feeding.

In terms of ego psychology all this shows a good deal of strengthening of the functions of the ego. The child has been enabled to perceive better, to understand better, and to control herself better. She has not lost her sense of identity through being in a strange environment. Rather it has been strengthened by her relationship with an accepting person. She has begun to be able to see the operation not as an attack on her but as something that can help her. There is movement from irrational fear to considered planning. The instinctual anxiety is less frightening and the reality of what is to be done is more clearly understood. Sue is beginning to realize that all these people are not hating her and attacking her but are attempting to help her realize her ambition of looking and feeling better, of 'becoming pretty'.

In spite of the amount of movement shown, Dr K decided after three weeks that it would be more risky to attempt surgery than to postpone it. He told Sue of the discharge plan, and she informed me of it when I went to see her that day. I told her I had not known of this and attempted to help her to express her feelings. When Dr K came into Sue's room, I told him that she wanted to go home for two weeks and then come back for the operation. A three-way discussion between surgeon, worker, and child took place, and Dr K took some time to explain to Sue that his reason for postponing the operation was that he felt it would work out better when she was a little older.

When he left she asked if I would come back to see her. I assured her that I would and that I would try to find someone else for her to talk with after she leaves the hospital, as she had been talking with me. We recognized together her confused feelings, her disappointment and her anger.

She was held over another day while the bands were removed from her teeth, and during that day she gave away all the things I had given her. Again I talked with her about her anger and accepted her feelings. By the time she left, she had gathered up most of the gifts again to take home.

After the amount of movement shown, the surgeon's decision to postpone the operation was disappointing to both the child and the caseworker, but he apparently believed that in spite of the child's improved morale as evidenced in her talking about the operation the risk of further failure was still too great. However, what we are concerned with here is the casework process. It is evident that the worker

H

finished her job by endeavouring to help the child work through her feelings of disappointment and anger at the postponement. One is left with a strong impression that the child's understanding of herself in relation to the major problem of her life was enhanced by these three weeks and that whatever might happen in the future the work with the child contributed to her ability to face an operation when it would eventually be performed.

This case is an interesting demonstration of casework help based on an understanding of ego psychology. There is no attempt to uncover the origins of the instinctual anxiety and anger the child shows in her biting and vomiting. The worker begins where the child is and helps her to work out her feelings about the immediate problem of the operation, never forcing her or pushing her unduly. Relationship remains warm, giving, purposeful. The worker's interpretations are at a simple level, related to the child's motivation and grasp. 'She is coming here to have the doctor fix her mouth so she will look better. She feels bad with it this way, and we all want to help her feel and look better.' The aim of casework here is not treatment of the child *per se* but rather treatment of a child in relation to facing a particular ordeal. Because the goal is realistic, related to modifying the child's feelings and behaviour about a stressful situation, such help may be seen to strengthen the ego's capacity to endure and adapt to frustration.

10

NOTES ON THE ROLE CONCEPT
IN CASEWORK WITH MOTHERS OF
BURNED CHILDREN*

JOAN M. WOODWARD

I HAVE found the role concept most helpful in working with mothers whose children come as in-patients to the burns unit of the Birmingham Accident Hospital.

In this setting there is a basic similarity in the problems, so that the main value of the role concept seems to be not so much in 'focusing the field of work' or 'finding a point of entry', but rather to enable the mothers to *understand* what is happening to their child and themselves. This understanding often leads to a better handling of the child, which in turn helps the mother to regain confidence in herself.

The idea that a mother should care for and protect her child (particularly if it is small), is deeply imbedded in the mother role. It is a concept that the mother fosters not only in her own mind but also in her child's. One small, but typical example of this occurs when a mother of a little child who has hurt itself says, 'Mummy will kiss it better'.

Most of the mothers I have met in the burns unit show ambivalent feelings towards their children. The negative side is rarely outwardly expressed, and of course varies in intensity. I think it is an important factor in producing guilt feelings that can reach an almost intolerable level. Sometimes, for example, mothers feel they cannot face visiting their child, because they feel so responsible for the harm that has been done.

When mothers feel as acutely frightened as this, they can be helped by a recognition and acceptance by the caseworker of this fear. Sympathetic support and encouragement and a real appreciation of the courage needed before the mother can visit helps as well. There

* Published in *The Almoner*, Vol. XIV, No. 2, May 1961.

is no place here for criticism, though helping a mother to concentrate on her child's need of her, and how much her presence can help him, generally enables the mother to visit her child within a few days.

Just how guilty parents feel can often be seen by the remarks they make in the early stages: Mrs P the mother of five boys, whose youngest, aged two, was burned by an electric fire, described how she felt after James had been rushed to hospital in the family car by his father. The police arrived, and soon told Mrs P that they could see the accident was not due to negligence and they would not take any further steps. Later, as Mrs P picked up the bits of James's skin from the carpet, she said she felt 'she *wanted* to go to prison, and what's more, *ought* to go'.

This feeling of being a failure in the protective aspect of the parental role affects fathers as well as mothers. A father whose little girl of seven had just been admitted said, speaking of the burns unit, 'But it is so *dreadful*, only neglectful parents have their children in here, and we are so careful'. I said that in fact this was not so—that many of the parents of burned children are more careful than the average, and that accidents sometimes happen in the best of homes. I discussed with them the things they could now do for Susan—visit her as often as possible, bring anything she specially liked from home, send her a letter or postcard each day—so that as far as possible they could go on playing the 'good father and mother role', which at the moment they felt they had failed in so badly.

When a burn accident occurs to a child, and he is rushed to hospital as an emergency admission, a swift change of roles occurs. He is no longer an ordinary child at home, in his normal safe-feeling environment, but he becomes, albeit temporarily, a 'patient in hospital'. Similarly his mother loses the immediate responsibility for her child by allowing the hospital to 'take over' and she takes on a new role of 'hospital visitor'. This rapid change of roles for both mother and child brings many new situations and new expectations. Often the vague idea of these roles—for example how a child behaves in hospital—does not match up with the reality.

I have found, that apart from the guilt feelings already described (which appear in different forms, sometimes over a period of years) the earliest difficulties that arise come from an inability to adapt to the new roles of 'patient' or 'visitor'. For example:

Michael, aged sixteen, burned both his feet when walking into hot ashes on a railway embankment, while train spotting with a boy friend. He is a highly intelligent boy, but according to his mother is usually quiet and not a 'good mixer'. The staff nurse reported to me that Michael was 'very strange and difficult' on the ward. Apparently he was due to sit his GCE examination the day after his accident. He was so agitated about missing it that arrangements were made by the consultant and nursing staff for Michael to be taken to the examination in a wheel chair. At the last moment, however, he refused to go, with the result that the staff concerned were pretty exasperated. I was told that from the time of his admission Michael insisted on having screens round his bed for all his meals and washing times, etc. On hearing all this I went at once to see him. I introduced myself by name, and said I was the social worker who was around to try and help anyone who felt worried. Michael gave a faint smile, and I asked him if he had ever been in hospital before. Michael said, 'No.' I then said that I guessed it all felt pretty strange and that it must have been a real shake up having an accident on the day before such an important exam. At my suggestion he then told me about the accident, expressing deep gratitude to his friend who apparently carried Michael to a first aid post.

I stayed with Michael, telling him that most people felt very shy when they first came into an open ward, but that really the other patients, though he would find them friendly, were not specially interested in him; they were thinking of their own troubles! At this Michael grinned and later accepted with obvious pleasure the offer of an egg for his tea from the man in the next bed. He ate this, without screens, while I stayed with him. During this time I was able to tell him a bit about the burns unit; the names of the nurses and doctors and other patients, and answered his questions about ward routine and procedure, etc. I left, telling him he had only to send a message to the almoners' department and I would come up any time. Later that evening I met Michael's parents. His father is an accountant. He spoke of his great hopes of Michael taking up accountancy and working in his office. His mother talked of how shy and sensitive Michael is, and gave as an explanation her own fearful experiences during the war when she was pregnant with Michael. Both his parents took a very protective attitude towards him.

I saw Michael nearly every day for the next fortnight. During these times he brought up many things he was worried about. For example, he was very concerned at being constipated, and too embarrassed to ask the nurses for a laxative. He was very alarmed at the sight of a plastic 'air-way' he saw in the mouth of a patient returning from the operating theatre. These and other fears all arose from things Michael did not know about, or felt unable to cope with, largely because he was in a strange setting. Talking about these fears seemed to help him at once either to understand and so feel less afraid, or to decide what he could do about them.

Michael's discharge came when I was on leave, but I met him and his mother a few weeks later in the outpatients' department. His mother said, out of his hearing, that his stay in hospital had changed him considerably. He was much less shy, generally more confident, and had a 'greater belief in the world's kindness'.

During a later visit to the hospital I was able to help Michael's mother make a decision about his playing games. The consultant said he considered Michael fit to play rugger. Michael, however, did not want to, and felt uncertain about hurling himself into such a tough game so soon. His mother was very indignant about what she felt was callousness on the part of the surgeon and his 'lack of understanding of what Michael had gone through'. I suggested that perhaps his mother knew Michael better than anyone, and that she and Michael could jointly see his headmaster and discuss possible alternatives to rugger that would be acceptable to Michael.

Later I heard by letter that he had chosen cross-country running 'at his own pace'. Michael wrote some weeks later to tell me of his excellent examination results, which he took at the end of the following term. The last I saw of Michael was in the surgeon's review clinic, when he told me he had gone into a bank in preference to his father's office. His mother said she was astonished at the way he had 'blossomed'. He is reading for his banking exams, and already has two 'juniors' working for him.

Michael is somewhat exceptional in the acuteness of his fears of the strangeness of hospital, but adolescents often seem the worst off in this respect. They cannot so easily cry and protest as a small child, and they do not have the knowledge and experience that most adults can fall back on to help them.

At a later stage, I have found the role concept has also proved most valuable in helping mothers to understand the problems that arise when they or their children cling to the idea that the burn and stay in hospital is a punishment of some sort.

When one examines the usual way that the role of a child is built up, it seems that from babyhood most children are taught to associate 'naughty behaviour' with unpleasant consequences. Most mothers even today, slap, shake or shout at their children when they disapprove of their behaviour. This generally hurts and frightens the child. Often threats such as 'I won't love you any more' or punishment such as being sent to bed or banishment to the bedroom are used.

When a burn accident happens, similar situations occur on a far greater scale. Not just one quick hurt of a slap, and the fright from a sudden cross voice, but often severe pain that is terrifying in its suddenness, followed by 'banishment' from home and perhaps weeks in bed. Unfortunately, in some cases these accidents do arise from children doing the very things that they have repeatedly been told not to do, and this just endorses the feeling that the accident is a punishment and evidence in the child's mind of rejection by its parents.

It is interesting to see how unobjective even adults are in this situation. Many mothers have said to me, 'I know I'm not always the best of mothers, but I didn't think I deserved *this* lot'. Similarly, quite a few have said, when referring to their child's accident, 'How can I believe in God when this happens?' This feeling of being lost and bewildered and no longer 'safe' in the world is sometimes most valuable when openly expressed, as one can help the mother to relate her own feelings with those of her child—he is asking virtually an identical question: 'How can I believe in Mummy's love for me when this happens?'

When these problems are discussed with the mothers in quite a straightforward way, most of them see that they have brought up their children to believe in the protective powers of their parents; that most little children are totally unaware of how limited these powers really are, and that when an accident happens there tends to be a shattering of the child's beliefs in both the parents' ability and desire to care for and love him.

I encourage mothers to talk about the kind of punishments they used before the accident, as this often leads to the mothers seeing for themselves why their child interprets the accident as a form of punishment. Mothers need help in understanding that the aggressive and demanding behaviour their children so often display when they return home, is not evidence of being 'spoilt' in hospital. It is a result not of *actual* parental rejection, but of the child feeling *as if it was*. Much of the aggressive behaviour that these children show on their return home seems to be a testing out to see just how much their mothers really do love them. A few mothers are able to go further still in their understanding and see some of the unconscious factors—such as the child's desire to be punished, and his fears about his own aggressive impulses and the associated fears of parental retaliation.

Jennifer was a child who showed typical signs of feeling that her accident and stay in hospital were evidence of rejection by her mother. She was the youngest of three girls. At the age of two, she bit through an electric cable and had a nasty burn of her mouth. She was only in the ward for nine days, but because of distance her parents could not visit every day. Jennifer was extremely subdued while in hospital. When seen in the out-patients' clinic some weeks after her discharge from the ward, Jennifer's mother said she was quite satisfied with her; but when seen again in the review clinic a few months later, her mother complained that she was having very bad nights, as Jennifer was waking with 'dreadful nightmares'.

As this sort of reaction is common and did not sound very serious, I suggested to Jennier's mother, Mrs K, that if she went on being patient and reassuring the nightmares would probably pass. Six months later I went to see Mrs K at home to hear how things were going. It was at once apparent that the situation had deteriorated. Unfortunately, since Jennifer returned home, her mother had been in hospital twice herself and was still unwell and awaiting a third visit. In spite of the fact that the father was at home during these occasions, Jennifer was showing typical symptoms of separation. Her mother described at length how Jennifer would not let her out of her sight, and if left, how she 'sobbed and screamed hysterically'. Jennifer was described as 'very naughty, disobedient, rather wild and insisting on having her own way'. Her mother spoke with real concern of Jennifer's endless demands for cakes, buns and sweets, etc., and how the child had become very fat. She had also returned to babyish ways, particularly over feeding and refused to use a knife and fork. Mrs K said she thought Jennifer's 'nerves were upset' as she was jumpy and quickly frightened—she mentioned how earlier that day an aeroplane had flown rather low over the house and Jennifer 'had screamed her head off'. At this point I asked Mrs K why she thought Jennifer was like this, and what she had already tried to do to help her. Mrs K said, very near to tears, that this was the 'whole trouble'—she said that *she* felt sure Jennifer was really frightened because she had been left by her mother three times—that she was not '*really* naughty'. Unfortunately, the in-laws were very strict, and kept calling Jennifer a 'baby'. If they are ever in charge of her they force her to use a knife and fork, etc. They slap her hard if she has a temper outburst. Once or twice when Mrs K had had to go out and the in-laws have put Jennifer to bed, there have been 'dreadful scenes'. Mrs K added, 'They are accusing me of spoiling her, and sometimes I wonder if I am doing the right thing, or whether *they* are really right.' I suggested to Mrs K the proof of the pudding was in the eating—and asked how the in-laws' tactics worked. Mrs K said at once Jennifer was always worse after she had been with them, and she felt sure Jennifer needed gentle handling. When Jennifer was alone with her parents and getting their full attention she was happy and a 'different child'. This led to a discussion of what Jennifer had been like before the accident, and how a child of two needs to be sure of her mother's loving presence. I suggested it must have felt 'like the end of the world' to Jennifer to be hurt and away in hospital, unable to have the usual comforting from her mother. When Mrs K said 'Jennifer seems to be cross with me, as though she was paying me out', I suggested Jennifer must have felt at two, that her mother was 'all powerful' and that therefore this sending Jennifer away from home would seem to have been done 'on purpose'—especially when the situation was virtually repeated twice again when her mother left her to go into hospital.

I suggested to Mrs K that really Jennifer's symptoms were a hopeful and positive sign of her attempts to regain her mother's love—she had not withdrawn and given up all hope of regaining it, like some children do, who feel completely abandoned. I agreed that for all that, Jennifer was not easy to manage, and she would need a lot of patience. The interview ended when Jennifer wanted to join in. Two later interviews were spent talking with Mrs K about the practical ways she felt she could help Jennifer. As Mrs K was convinced by this time that Jennifer's difficulties were largely based on a *belief* that her mother had rejected her (as distinct from the actual fact) it became possible to talk over ways of reassuring Jennifer that her mother's love for her remained unchanged, if Jennifer or her mother had to go to hospital. I suggested to Mrs K she might get this idea across in the form of a story: (How a little girl got burned, how sorry her mother was, how she visited, took presents, etc., and longed to have her home. How sometimes the little girl gets very cross and upset, that she feels the accident was her mummy's fault and that she didn't love her, but this is not so, etc., etc.) Mrs K seemed very intrigued to try this, and realized she might have to try various versions on different occasions.

I heard in a later interview that Jennifer had listened very solemnly and then said, 'No, it was Miranda's fault (her big sister), *she* should have kept me away from the wire.' She then paused and asked, 'Who told you to tell me that story?' Her mother laughed as she described this, and seemed proud of Jennifer's understanding. The story was apparently asked for again, and led to an interesting discussion of why Jennifer put the blame on Miranda.

This little girl is verbally very precocious, and her mother feels she will do very well when she gets to school. In some ways she seems ready for school now, but she cannot be accepted until she is five. All Jennifer's compulsive eating has now disappeared. She often suggests being left with neighbour's children while her mother goes out shopping, etc. She has far fewer temper outbursts and is altogether easier and more relaxed. She had a 'relapse' on all these improvements when she was ill for three weeks with food poisoning, but she has caught up again. This made her mother realize that Jennifer's hold on these achievements is as yet somewhat slender, and it may take a while to consolidate them, but Mrs K is now quite convinced she is on the right track. The last time I saw Mrs K she said she could hardly believe it, the in-laws had commented that Jennifer was getting to be 'a nice little girl again'.

This seems to be a case where the mother understood and saw Jennifer's needs, but needed support herself in carrying them through against opposition from relatives that might have got her down and proved disastrous for Jennifer.

One of the most frequently met difficulties for children who have been in hospital is that of accepting a less important role when the crisis is over.

An appreciation of why this might be, on the part of the mother, helps to replace the usual comment that 'so-and-so is spoilt, and just wants his own way', with an understanding of the child's real feelings that enables the mother to help her child.

Derek was a little boy of five who went home after a severe scald of the chest. Some weeks after discharge he kept complaining of 'feeling sick'. He went pale but never actually vomited. These feelings occurred five or six times a day but seemed unconnected with meals or any other obvious cause. His mother was a Jehovah's Witness and reluctant to take the boy to the doctor. I suggested Derek might be missing the attentions he had when all the family's anxieties were centred on him. His mother later appreciated that this was so, when her little girl was ill and Derek openly commented that he 'wished he was poorly'. She was able to help him feel life was more fun when he was well, and the sick feelings soon passed.

Sometimes it is the parents who find difficulties in letting go the idea that their child still needs 'invalid treatment' many months after the child's return home.

Jane's parents completely disagreed about the way she should be treated. At the age of five she had had a very severe burn which endangered her life, and left her with bad scars, some of which were on her face. When she returned home she at once became very aggressive and demanding—screaming, hitting, stamping and sobbing. Her mother was a rather nervous, but patient little woman, who quietly but firmly showed Jane what she expected of her.

Jane's father was out of work and at home for many weeks after the child's discharge. He had upbraided his wife quite mercilessly over the accident in the first place and was for ever 'rubbing it in', how it had been 'her fault' and what a 'neglectful mother' she was. In point of fact, this was very far from the truth.

Once Jane was home, her father insisted that she had had such a 'terrible time' that everyone must now 'make it up to her'. She was to be allowed to do everything and anything she wanted, regardless of her brothers and sisters. He insisted that his wife was being 'cruel' to Jane when she made the child go up to bed at a normal time, take her turn in games with the others, etc.

Fortunately, Jane's father eventually started work and her mother was left in sole charge except on Sundays. Almost immediately Jane's demands and tears came to manageable proportions. She started school and the tension in the household began to ease.

This mother was able to express quite clearly, after a few interviews, that her husband's attitude was making Jane worse, because he reacted as though Jane's fears were real and her demands reasonable. Jane's mother saw that if she expected and allowed Jane to behave quite differently because of her burn, the child would begin to think differently about herself. Although this is an over-simplification of the situation, talking about it in this way did enable this mother to cope with Jane in a very consistent manner and helped to make Jane feel she knew where she was. Interestingly enough, it also enabled her mother to explain to neighbours and relatives what she was about when they commented that she was being 'hard' on Jane.

The most complicated problems of all seem to arise with children who have a great fear of being damaged. It may be that they have already had a previous accident; or they may have been struggling with marked castration anxieties which the burn accident then seems to touch off. If this occurs when the burn is quite small, the mother tends to feel that the child's reaction is out of all proportion to the accident.

Sylvia was seven, and the elder of two children. Her nightdress caught fire, which resulted in burns of her abdomen and thighs. These were not serious and did not require grafting.

Sylvia was very miserable at the beginning of her stay in hospital, and one of the first things she told me was that the accident was her young brother's fault as she said he removed the fireguard. Sylvia was in hospital for just over a week, and treated as an outpatient for four or five weeks after this. During this time I got to know her mother who seemed a sensitive but sensible woman, fond of both her children, but rather uncertain about how to deal with them.

Less than a month after Sylvia's discharge from the ward I went to see her mother, Mrs M, at home. It was only possible to have a short talk out of Sylvia's hearing, and it seemed Mrs M's anxieties were considerable. She described Sylvia as 'changed', restless, quite wild, not sleeping properly—waking in the night and screaming; on two occasions she had walked in her sleep. She had lost her appetite and was apparently so nervous that she did not like her mother to leave her, even to go to the lavatory which was outside in the yard. Sylvia appeared at this point in the interview, so I said to her and her mother that most children feel a bit upset and frightened after the sort of experience Sylvia had had, but that she would feel happier again before long. I reminded Mrs M of the talks we had had in the hospital and promised to be around so that we could talk more fully later.

A week later we met in the outpatients' clinic, as arranged; Sylvia was considered fit for school, and another meeting was then agreed on between Mrs M and myself. At the start of this next visit it became clear that Mrs M was really aghast at Sylvia's behaviour. She had great fears that the child was 'queer'. She was still sleeping badly, aggressive in behaviour and 'showing off', but her mother was most worried by various incidents that seemed to her very strange. Apparently on one occasion Sylvia's dog caught his tail in the fire: she grabbed hold of him and said, 'Good, I'm glad you've got burned too—I hope it hurt.' As Mrs M recounted this, she said it shocked her that Sylvia could have such ideas. On Mothering Sunday, Sylvia gave her mother a bunch of daffodils. She had wrapped the stalks up in a bandage: when her mother started to remove this Sylvia apparently became quite hysterical and insisted it must stay on. She also insisted the flowers were to be put in a glass vase so that the bandage could be seen.

It seemed too soon to suggest at this stage the probable reason why Sylvia should so relish her male dog getting his tail burned; but we did talk about her 'spiteful' feelings that were directed towards the dog and other children being a sign of her need for reassurance.

Mrs M began to see that Sylvia was probably giving the bandaged flowers as a representation of herself, and this led on to Mrs M describing how persistent Sylvia had been lately in giving her mother presents—sometimes three or four a day.

I asked Mrs M what she thought were the reasons why Sylvia might want to give her a lot of presents. At first she spoke of Sylvia's love and gratitude, and then got on to the idea of Sylvia feeling the need to placate her mother, and we spoke of the possible fantasies behind this. As we talked, through the next few interviews, it became clear that Mrs M badly wanted to understand Sylvia and help her, but felt at times at a loss how to do so. She spoke of an earlier time when Sylvia was a baby—how she had great difficulties with feeding, and had longed to have someone to turn to then. She seemed appreciative of the bargain we had made, that together we would try to understand why Sylvia behaved as she did, and work out what could be done about it. A lot of discussion centred on the difference between the roles of girl and boy, first born and second child, and why Sylvia and her younger brother were so different.

It soon became apparent that Sylvia was continuously pushing herself forward, could not bear it if she was not constantly praised. She said she had good marks at school when this was not so. This led to Mrs M seeing, apparently for the first time, just how jealous Sylvia was of her brother. Sylvia still seemed over-excited, very restless, quite unable to talk slowly or to sit still. Her mother noticed that she seemed compelled to challenge every situation. She would, for example, over-excite the dog until she drove him to bite her. She was at this time having nightmares about spiders crawling over her, and of sinking into quicksands.

Her mother complained of Sylvia being 'nosey'—searching into drawers, being too forthright with friends and neighbours and earning a reputation of being 'rude'. On one occasion she took a bottle of perfume from the house of one of her mother's friends.

It now seemed so obvious that Sylvia was very worried about her apparent sexual inferiority in comparison with her brother, that I suggested this was at the back of much of her behaviour. It only took a burst of sexual questions from Sylvia to convince her mother that this was so. Mrs M changed her policy of avoiding giving answers, to telling Sylvia about babies, and reassuring her that her own sex organs were whole and safe inside her. At the same time she allowed Sylvia to play a game of being 'baby' that she often had asked for but had previously been denied. This involved being cuddled on her mother's lap, with 'pretend' bottle feeds and nappy changing.

Mrs M also arranged for the younger boy to go to bed half an hour earlier than Sylvia, so that she and her mother had this time together before her father came in. This was known as 'Sylvia's time', and she told her mother during one of these sessions how pleased she was her mother had told her 'the secret about babies'.

With Mrs M's agreement, I also went to see Sylvia's class teacher, and she began to give Sylvia some extra jobs in the classroom. Within a few weeks Sylvia began to bring real 'good marks' home from school. She slept better, and the sleep walking and nightmares stopped. The most noticeable change was her ability to sit still and concentrate. She started knitting and painting, which she had been much too restless to do before.

Her mother brought up with me her own anxieties about mental illness, that partly arose as a result of a next-door neighbour going into a mental hospital. This woman often stayed long periods in Mrs M's house. This led to a discussion of the importance of trying to help children with their problems at an early stage, and I linked this with Mrs M's earlier fears of Sylvia's 'queerness'.

Mrs M is showing a great satisfaction in helping Sylvia and she enjoys the child's growing identification with her. This mother has grasped with surprising rapidity some of the reasons why Sylvia had such a marked reaction to her accident, and this understanding has enabled her to help Sylvia with considerable success.

In conclusion, I would like to emphasize that the use of the role concept has not led me to work in a radically different way, but it has helped me to clarify situations with these mothers, and to do so in everyday language that has some meaning to them.

11

SOCIAL DETERMINANTS OF FAMILY BEHAVIOUR*

OTTO POLLAK

BEFORE we can identify social factors that determine the behaviour of family members towards one another, or towards the outside world, it would seem appropriate to clarify two important concepts, namely, the use of the term 'social' and the lack of a precise referent for the word 'family'.

In social work theory the term 'social' is frequently juxtaposed with the term 'psychological', or treated as if social and psychological considerations would have to be combined for a complete understanding of human behaviour. The psychological is usually seen as internal to the individual, the social as external. Although basically correct, this suggests that the social has no psychological elements, which can easily lead to a disregard of relevant phenomena in the social sphere surrounding an individual. If we stop to consider that the *human* environment of an individual is composed of individuals, we quickly realize that the *social* environment of a human being is composed of the psyches of other human beings. A meaningful discussion of social determinants will therefore have to include psychological elements.

The concept of the family also requires a measure of analysis. The problem here is created by the fact that all families have a basic structure of blood relationships and that in some instances people who are not blood related share a home with those who are, whereas other blood-related family members do not.

In the United States we are accustomed to assume that parents and children normally live together and that in consequence the family of procreation (the nuclear family) coincides with the 'family of orientation' as far as the children are concerned. When a parent is absent

* Published in *Social Work*, Vol. VIII, No. 3, July 1963.

from this unit because of death, desertion, or divorce we speak of a 'broken family', designating a deficit in normal family membership. On the other hand, when relatives belonging to a wider circle of kinship (grandmothers, aunts, or cousins, for example) share the home we are quickly inclined to think of excess membership and feel that we must extend the concept of the family of orientation to these persons. Actually, study has shown that even strangers who share the home may play such a role in a child's developmental experiences that they should be considered members of the family of orientation.[1] From a diagnostic and therapeutic point of view, the concept of the 'family of orientation' is useful because it attracts the attention of clinicians to people who may play a role in a child's developmental experiences, but who are overlooked because they do not belong to the nuclear family.[2]

Another social science concept may be useful in helping clinicians accept psychological conceptions of the family that are smaller than the total family of procreation. Reference is here made to the concept of 'life space', which identifies as significant only those parts of the human environment of an individual that have dynamic meaning for him, that is, people who he perceives and evaluates.[3] The family in the actual life space of an individual may be smaller than the number of people whom a medical social worker, for instance, would consider actual members of a patient's family. Many records of medical social workers contain references to blood-related relatives who do not behave as if they were members of the patient's family. On the other hand, a patient might not accept as a possible resource in home care a family member whom the medical social worker would find capable and appropriate to render such service.[4]

The various configurations of possible family meaning for patient and social worker suggest the need for a more functional—and at the same time more adaptable—definition of the family than we encounter in the literature. The writer would like to suggest that *a family exists when people related to one another either by blood or the sharing of a home consider themselves resources for one another on a more comprehensive basis and at higher degree of intensity than they consider other*

[1] James H. S. Bossard, *The Sociology of Child Development*, Harper & Bros., New York, 1948, pp. 59-60.
[2] Otto Pollak, 'A Family Diagnosis Model', *Social Service Review*, Vol. XXXIV, No. 1, March 1960, pp. 19-31, especially p. 23.
[3] Kurt Levin, 'Environmental Forces', in Carl Murchison, ed., *Child Psychology*, Clark University Press, Worcester, Mass., 1933, pp. 594-5.
[4] Otto Pollak, 'Cultural Factors Encountered in Patients, Part II', *Medical Social Work*, Vol. III, No. 4, October 1954, pp. 139-52, especially pp. 147-8.

people. A mother may be separated from her adult son by a geographic distance of 3,000 miles, yet consider herself entitled to his emotional and financial support far beyond what she would expect from anybody else. Another mother may live on the same block with her adult son and prefer to share her problems with, and receive help from, a neighbour rather than her son. Two friends who share a home may form a functional system as a family in terms of human resource readiness for, and human resource demand upon, each other.

Family closeness is not fully determined by either proximity or blood relationship. Once this is realized and a family ceases to be defined by either the common housing basis of a shared apartment or dwelling or by blood relationship in ascending and descending order, we have a working concept which will identify for family members and social workers alike just *who* can be counted upon for co-operation in home care planning for a patient. To extend the family circle *ad hoc* by attempting to change attitudes of unconcern into attitudes of willingness to serve as a family resource is an unpromising task and probably beyond the time and relationship potential of social work.

Social work is a democratic profession, at least in its concepts of appropriate family behaviour. Consequently, social workers are inclined to relate their observations of power concentration in a specific family member to pathology. In practically every clinical discussion reference is made to a domineering mother figure and a passive father. Correction workers are concerned with powerless parents, and social workers who deal with recent immigrants are concerned with a patriarchal arrangement and a double standard for men and women.

Actually, power concentration in one member of the family or another is not an expression of pathology, but is usually an expression of the history, religion, and ethnology of a population group. Members of the American working class usually live under patriarchal arrangements because they frequently stem from a background that is predominantly Catholic, farm, and/or Latin.[1] The mother, or sometimes the grandmother, in Negro families of rural Southern background is likely to behave as a true matriarch,[2] and the urban middle-class family in our society is said to move towards 'companionship',[3] i.e. towards

---

[1] S. M. Miller and Frank Riessman, 'The Working Class Sub-Culture: A New View', *Social Problems,* Vol. IX, No. 1, Summer 1961, pp. 86–97.
[2] Franklin Frazier, *The Negro Family in the United States,* University of Chicago Press, 1939.
[3] Ernest W. Burgess and Harvey J. Locke, *The Family From Institution to Companionship,* 2nd. ed., American Book Company, New York, 1953, p. 24.

I

an egalitarian structure (which, however, tends toward a matriarchal arrangement because the father's occupation frequently requires his absence from the home[1]). Another family with matriarchal structure is the Jewish family, which has a long history of social powerlessness of the male and has developed a mother dominance echoing centuries of experience that required this form of adaptation to a hostile environment.[2]

From the viewpoint of social work, the power structure in a specific population group may have two relevant aspects. (1) When a family structure shows power concentration in a person who according to the culture of his group should not be expected to have such power, we are likely to have a case of family pathology. (2) If the patient is the power person in the family, the social worker must evaluate the family constellation and ascertain whether somebody stepped into the vacuum created, for example, by the patient's hospitalization or whether the family has subsequently failed to reorganize itself.

If a new power nucleus is in formation, planning will have to connect with this new nucleus; if the family has remained without a new power nucleus, then it will have to be helped to restructure itself, or the patient may have to be made the counterpart of the social worker in planning post hospital arrangements. This latter situation might present a delicate situation because the hospital atmosphere is conducive to regression and the active planning of post medical care requires either recovery from regression or rejection of regression in the first place. In this case communication between social worker and nursing staff, or possibly doctors, may be essential in order to create a therapeutic environment in which post medical care can be planned and successfully carried on.

It has been pointed out by Parsons and Fox that in the American culture illness absolves people from the normal functions demanded of them by society. This relief from social obligations has been found to be a significant secondary gain in many cases of illness. At the same time, they point out, the limitation in membership and facilities of the modern American family forces more and more sick people into hospital care and thus counteracts the secondary gain of relief from social obligations.[3]

[1] Otto Pollak, 'Interrelationships Between Economic Institutions and the Family', *Social Security Bulletin*, Vol. XXIII, No. 10, October 1960, pp. 10-12.

[2] Mark Zborowski and Elizabeth Herzog, *Life is with People: The Jewish Little-Town of Eastern Europe*, International Universities Press, New York, 1952.

[3] Talcott Parsons and Renee C. Fox, 'Illness, Therapy, and the Modern Urban American Family', in Norman W. Bell and Ezra F. Vogel, eds., *The Family*, The Free Press, Glencoe, Ill., 1960, p. 351.

To medical social workers this might easily appear to be an over-simplification. Actually the hospital might represent for the patient a refuge from the tension of family conflict and, by its regression-inducing atmosphere, reinforce the psychological gains derived from the release from social responsibilities. Consequently, for certain patients hospitalization cannot be presumed to be an ambivalent experience. The task of medical social work, then, is to concern itself with the psychological meaning of hospitalization as an escape from family life just as much as it does with the disruptive effect of a patient's hospitalization on his family. Particularly in a culture in which character disorders and accompanying depression occur with increasing frequency, the hospital may appear more and more as a refuge of the depressed. In the light of family constellations that might arise under the impact of illness upon patients with character disorders, the traditional division of labour between medical staff and social service staff may appear obsolete. Post hospital care may require just as much, if not more, preparatory work with the patient than with his family, something which is recognized in modern rehabilitation practice but probably requires extension to other areas of hospital treatment.[1]

A prominent social value in American family life is the general release of children from obligations toward their parents. Short of growing up normally, very little is demanded of American children. In part this is because modern living arrangements furnish fewer opportunities for children to be useful to their parents than existed in earlier times. Partly, too, parents have come to believe that to demand services from their children is somewhat unethical, that children should be paid if they do work for them, and that the ultimate purpose of child rearing is separation—emotionally, occupationally, and geographically—between parent and child.[2]

Such conditions give rise to a rift between adult sons and daughters and their ageing parents, so that when the latter become ill the demands upon the former somehow interfere with normal and appropriate arrangements. Illness in the young will bring quick response because the normal resources will be parents, and parents (unless emotionally conflicted) accept this responsibility without question. No such

[1] Otto Fenichel, *The Psychoanalytic Theory of Neurosis*, W. W. Norton & Co., New York, 1945, p. 464; Otto Pollak, Hazel M. Young and Helen Leach, 'Differential Diagnosis and Treatment of Character Disturbances', *Social Casework*, Vol. XXXXI, No. 10, December 1960, pp. 512-17.
[2] Erik H. Erikson, *Childhood and Society*, W. W. Norton & Co., New York, 1950, pp. 244-83.

stimulus exists for an adult son and daughter when the parent becomes ill, and this cultural situation between generations will present many difficulties in planning post hospital care.[1]

The family is a social organization representing a working system of living and development among people of different sex and different stages of physical and mental maturity. Like other social systems of larger scale, it requires norms of behaviour which in the last analysis represent an expression of the victory of the reality principle over the pleasure principle. People give up—and must give up—gratification in the present for gratification in the future. They must learn to restrain their impulses in the service of life maintenance and the rearing of future generations. They must submit to norms in order to gain the benefits of maturation and development and mutual protection.

In the battle between impulse and social norms, those who learn to accept the norms must sometimes pay the price of partial incapacitation or anxiety. The principles and successes of psychoanalytically oriented helping efforts have been developed and achieved in the treatment of these conditions, the neuroses. Strangely enough, the clients who represent the greatest challenge to social work and the wider community at the present time do not suffer from the scars of submitting to the reality principle—they suffer from the ineffectiveness of having retained the pleasure principle as a guide of living. They lead a life of normlessness, conceptualized by Merton as anomie.[2]

For people who are victims of anomie—and this includes mothers on public relief as well as playboys—we have no theory of helping, no tradition of success. Social work and psychiatry are without appropriate armamentarium because the helping professions have learned essentially only how to liberate people who have become beneficiaries, of a norm-directed life. Social work is here faced with the challenge of becoming a rearing, binding, superego-demanding profession rather than of being a liberating one.[3] In order to do so, however, it has to free itself from the frequent misconception that to belong to an economically disadvantaged social class is the same phenomenon as anomie. A person who is integrated in the class structure always has values for life in the future to which he sacrifices

[1] John Sirjamaki, 'Cultural Configurations in the American Family', in Bell and Vogel, op. cit., p. 299.

[2] Robert K. Merton, Social Theory and Social Structure, rev. ed., The Free Press, Glencoe, Ill., 1957, pp. 131-94.

[3] Otto Pollak, 'Treatment of Character Disorders: A Dilemma in Casework Culture', Social Service Review, Vol. XXXV, No. 2, June 1961.

gratification in the present. His future goals may vary from class to class, but their attainment is always governed by the reality principle. People who live in anomie may be destitute, sick, and needful but they are not integrated in any of the existing classes in our society. Here social workers will have come to terms with a phenomenon of normlessness which makes liberating or improving efforts miss the mark. What social science can contribute, then, is to point out that classes are different ways of life which, no matter how different, are governed by norms. To help people with normlessness, however, is a new challenge.

No helping effort can succeed without support by society—or at least a significant part of society—for appropriate motivation in the client. In this respect the increasing numbers of middle-class clients present a problem for the social worker. One of the greatest life-maintaining and mobilization-promoting influences is ambition for the future. Such ambition comes easily in a society in which relatively few have attained affluence but opportunity seems open to many. In a society in which affluence have been achieved by many, however, the impetus of expectation fades.

One of the most significant studies in this respect deals with the attitudes of middle-class fathers regarding the future of their children. According to this study, the concern of middle-class fathers is not to see their sons attain more than they have attained, but mild anxiety over whether their sons will attain as much as they have.[1] In other words, an aggressive stance towards the future is turned into a conservative stance. Conservatism, however, is not buoyant—it cannot gain from the expectation of a better future the strength necessary to cope with the present.

Similar study of white people in the working classes reveals that they, too, show little ambition for the social improvement of their children.[2] Actually, it is more the Negro who, particularly via the opportunities provided by government service, still shows ambition for the transition from lower-class to middle-class status and the concomitant emotional stance of optimism. If a Negro rises from lower-class to middle-class status he does this not only for himself, but feels that he thereby also serves the status of his group. The writer suspects that even the Negro delinquent has the push of a related social motivation—he may feel himself to be a fighter against con-

---

[1] David F. Aberle and Kaspar D. Naegele, 'Middle-Class Fathers' Occupational Role and Attitudes toward Children', in Bell and Vogel, op. cit., pp. 126-36.
[2] Miller and Riessman, op. cit.

ditions of social injustice, a challenger of the suppressor, and thus in the last analysis a servant of his group.

In other words, social workers will find in many Negro clients, if they do not live under conditions of anomie, a hopeful attitude towards the future that they will not similarly find among white people. This stance of optimism, however, did exist in the social climate of white clients until fairly recently and is still presumed to exist by donors, the general public, and the allied professions of social work, if not by social workers themselves. Here social work theory and social work practice will have to develop new orientations and conceivably new philosophical goals for white clients in order to create conditions under which a helping effort has a reasonable chance to succeed.

Ever since psychoanalysis and psychoanalytically oriented social work captured the attention of the helping professions, it has been realized that verbal communication on a fairly sophisticated level is a preferential condition for the selection of clients or patients and their successful treatment. The work of Hollingshead and Redlich has brought this into focus and has elucidated the privileged situation of psychiatry vs. social work in the power of selection of people for this type of help.[1]

In a society in which mass contribution of all services is considered a desirable social arrangement, however, such phenomena of bias in client selection and therapy represent a challenge that the helping professions will have to face. Since it is always the burdensome privilege of the less favoured to become pioneers it is very likely that, as between psychiatrist and social worker, social workers will come to terms with this challenge first. This will necessarily involve a great deal of experimentation with non verbal communication in therapy and with translation of professional terminology into the traditional language of clients.

Here another phenomenon will present specific difficulties. Because of the advances of technology, fewer and fewer people with limited mental endowment will have an opportunity to gain a measure of self-respect by self-support. They will have less and less experience in communication through socially useful activity. What will have to be developed is not only skill in non verbal communication but increasing skill in communication with dependent people that is no longer predicated on the silent assumption that independence should

[1] August B. Hollingshead and Fredrick C. Redlich, *Social Class and Mental Illness*, John Wiley & Sons, New York, 1958.

be the treatment goal. This is a demand of our time not yet recognized in either social security or in vocational rehabilitation. The age of automation will require not only a transition of communication from the verbal to the non verbal but a reorientation of assumed goals.[1]

It is, however, not only the power to communicate and the underlying assumptions about the desirability of independence that at present make different strata of society differently accessible to social work help—it is also the traditions of the past. These traditions have produced different attitudes towards welfare services and towards the responses which they require. It can safely be said that the attitude of Anglo-Saxons toward charitable help is that one should not need it, but that if one does one should not be required to show one's feelings about needing it. Since social work must proceed on the assumption of the respectability of needfulness and of the therapeutic desirability of expression of feelings, it can be assumed that social worker and Anglo-Saxon client initially will be less in accord than, for instance, the social worker and the client of Latin origin who believes in free expression of emotions and traditionally relates to dependence as an acceptable way of life.

With Jewish clients, however, the opposite relationship is likely to exist. While the Anglo-Saxon client may be reluctant to admit to himself his needfulness and while the Latin client may accept his needfulness with a measure of humility, the Jewish client is likely to demand relief with the stance of a social debt collector. This is partly based on the ethical prescriptions of the Bible which demand that the landowner leave one-tenth of his harvest to the poor, and partly because of the relationship between the two dominant Jewish classes, the scholars and the businessmen. In this class system wealth has been associated with lower-class status and scholarship with higher-class status. The scholar, even when dependent for his support on the wealthy, has always been accepted as superior to the businessman, and this has generalized itself into an aggressive custom of demanding welfare services when needed. Social workers, even those of Jewish background, frequently find this hard to take because they operate in a society with a value orientation that favours the donor and not the recipient.

All these differences in attitude toward charity result in differences in accessibility of various client groups to the helping potential of social work. These differences present in turn a task for social work

[1] F. H. George, *Automation, Cybernetics and Society*, Philosophical Library, New York, 1959, pp. 264-70.

that is culture-creating rather than culture-adapting. The implied change of culture will affect the wider community. It is too early to say what the characteristics of this coming service culture will be, but it can be predicted with a certain amount of assurance that needfulness will more and more become recognized as an acceptable way of existence, not only in times of crisis; that ability to use help will be recognized as superior to immobilization, not only by social workers but also by laymen; and that effectiveness of communication will become the determinant of the methods used rather than the prestige connotation of certain types of therapy.

12

A FAMILY DIAGNOSIS MODEL*

OTTO POLLAK

SOCIAL practitioners can meet the challenge of complexity in human relations only by simplifications that do not sacrifice coverage. When the focus of concern is a family, diagnostic understanding must be expressed in terms that cover all family members. Otherwise, attempts at simplification turn into falsifications and thus into threats to the effectiveness of the helping effort. It has been observed that on occasion as mother and child get better father gets worse.[1] Similarly, improvement in a child as a result of therapeutic effort has been known to be followed by the appearance of developmental problems in a brother or sister.[2] Promotion or restoration of family health in functional, and psychological terms thus present problems which require special diagnostic concepts formulated to make the task manageable for social caseworkers and therapists from other disciplines engaged in such services. Over and beyond the necessity of such concepts for the effectiveness of the helping effort, their provision must be demanded also from the point of view of the practitioner. It should not be forgotten that, at least in our culture, helping is a process which must gratify the need of the helper for the experience of professional adequacy just as much as the needs of his clients for improvement.

As far as I am able to gather from the professional literature and the study of case records, these concept requirements of a helping effort with a family focus have not yet been fully met. Dichotomies such as 'the client and his family' or 'the client and his environment' almost force the worker to concentrate on one person and to leave

* Published in The Social Service Review, Vol. XXXIV, No. 1, March 1960.
[1] Mildred Burgum, 'The Father Gets Worse: A Child Guidance Problem', American Journal of Orthopsychiatry, Vol. XII, July 1942, 474.
[2] Gordon Hamilton, Psychotherapy in Child Guidance, Columbia University Press, New York, 1947, p. 282.

family associates or other significant persons in the client's life-space either unconsidered or only dimly and selectively perceived.[1] Such dichotomies combine a concept representing one person with a concept representing several persons. They refer, however, to the concept representing a plurality—the family—in the singular and give thereby an impression of simplicity which can be translated into practice only by a fractionalization of reality. Thus parents become referred to as 'the parent' and practice descriptions reflect this singularization of pluralities quite frequently without any implication of awareness that this usage permits and actually justifies the exclusion of one of the two most important persons in a child's life.[2] In the end the singularization of pluralities in theory and practice creates the need for specific justification, and we find the parent who is taken into treatment referred to as 'the significant parent'.[3] Such usage implies that there must be also an insignificant parent—a proposition which upon reflection no social worker or psychiatrist would find acceptable.

A special difficulty in family casework and child placement lies in the frequency of cultural unrelatedness between caseworker and client. People who bring their children to child-guidance clinics usually have both an emotional affinity for and also some intellectual awareness of the professional culture of the therapists whom they are going to meet. They speak the same class language as the therapists and approach the helping experience with at least some terminological equipment.[4] The clients of family-service and child-placing agencies, however, are frequently separated from the culture of social workers not only by unfamiliarity with the essentials of the casework process but also by a class and ethnic gulf. In consequence they lack a common frame of reference with their workers and are frequently restricted to communicating with them by the expression of tones of feeling rather than by means of appropriate words. Furthermore, they frequently bring into the casework process notions of family health which are divergent if not contradictory to those held by the caseworker. In such instances, the helping process must assume a certain quality of acculturation in which the worker tries to help the client move at least

---

[1] Otto Pollak, *Integrating Sociological and Psychoanalytic Concepts: An Exploration in Child Psychotherapy*, Russell Sage Foundation, New York, 1956, pp. 198-201.

[2] Frederick Harold Allen, M.D., *Psychotherapy with Children*, W. W. Norton & Co., New York, 1942, pp. 10 et passim.

[3] Stanislaus Szurek, M.D., Adelaide Johnson, M.D. and Eugene Falstein, M.D., 'Collaborative Psychiatric Therapy of Parent-Child Problems', *American Journal of Orthopsychiatry*, Vol. XII, July 1942, 511.

[4] August B. Hollingshead and Frederick C. Redlich, M.D., *Social Class and Mental Illness*, John Wiley & Sons, New York, 1958, pp. 339-40.

somewhat in the direction of the mental health culture which the family-service and child-welfare fields in our society represent.[1] In order to do so planfully, however, the worker must have particular clarity about the nature of family structure and family functions which in this culture are held to be desirable.

Fortunately, several efforts have already been made to deal with these concerns. The persistent and insightful explorations of Dr Nathan W. Ackerman come quickly to mind.[2] In the field of cultural difference in family dynamics the work of Dr John P. Spiegel and Florence R. Kluckhohn have become widely known.[3] Recently Dr Martin Grotjahn has called for the development of analytic family therapy which would combine 'the experience and wisdom of the old-fashioned family physician with the skill and knowledge of a psychoanalyst.[4]

The particular efforts with which I have become connected are the result of a convergence between two developments: the liaison between social science and social work inaugurated by the Russell Sage Foundation,[5] and the concern of the Family Service Association of America with the consideration and study of the topics already highlighted above. As is altogether proper, this trend of concern for the improvement potential of family service has not remained the reserve of the initiating foundation but has found new sponsorship in the conference sponsored by the Elizabeth McCormick Memorial Fund,[6] which has encouraged further work in the development of a practical scheme of family diagnosis and family therapy. I have been asked to present a report on the results of my own work. These efforts have their origin in the work which I was called upon to do for the Jewish Board of Guardians and the Russell Sage Foundation.[7] They were carried on and have achieved whatever measure of crystalization they now have in two FSAA seminars at Lake Forest and in one seminar at the Family and Children's Service of Pittsburgh. Valuable experience has come my way also from Family Service of Philadelphia through

[1] Otto Pollak, 'Cultural Dynamics in Casework', *Social Casework*, Vol. XXXIV, July 1953, 284.

[2] Nathan W. Ackerman, M.D., *The Psychodynamics of Family Life: Diagnosis and Treatment*, Basic Books, New York, 1958.

[3] Group for the Advancement of Psychiatry, *Integration and Conflict in Family Behavior*, Report No. 27, Topeka, Kansas: GAP, August 1954.

[4] Martin Grotjahn, M.D., 'Analytic Family Therapy: A Survey of Trends in Research and Practice', in *Individual and Family Dynamics*, ed. Jules H. Masserman, M.D., Grune & Stratton, New York, 1959, p. 101.

[5] Russell Sage Foundation, New York, *Annual Report 1947-48*, pp. 13-14.

[6] 'Family Casework in the Interest of Children', *Social Casework*, Vol. XXXIX, February-March 1958, 59-182.

[7] Russell Sage Foundation, *Annual Report 1948-49*, pp. 13-14.

work on a model of healthy family relationships which was developed there.[1]

I should like to propose that one of the major premises for the formulation of a family diagnosis is the readiness of the worker to accept as his client the family group rather than an individual member. This is necessary not merely in order to protect treatment success in one individual against negative repercussions on the part of family members with whom he shares the home. Its justification is not even exhausted by a concern to extend the helping effort directly or indirectly to all members of the family who suffer from pathology. It is dictated in the last analysis by our concern for socially adaptive ego development of the children in the family and for that of their children in turn. Ego development cannot be understood in terms of only one interpersonal relationship, however strategically placed in the life-history of an individual. It has to be visualized at least in part as an effort of family-model combination.[2] In order to understand the nature of this combination we must understand the persons who have served and are serving as models, i.e. all the family members. This does not preclude a later treatment decision to work with only one or two members of the family group. The doctor now accepts the whole organism as his patient even if he decides to treat only locally. Similarly, caseworkers and family therapists from other disciplines must be willing to be concerned with the condition and improvement of the whole family group before making treatment decisions.

Another premise is the acceptance of the proposition that the object of diagnostic and therapeutic concern in family casework is the system of interpersonal relationships between the family members rather than the specific discomforts experienced by one person or the other. These relationships will have to be evaluated in terms of functional efficiency for the satisfaction of the present needs of the individuals involved and in terms of the impact which these relationships are likely to exercise on the future ability of these individuals to form other relationships. Incidentally, it might be stated that this second premise has an implication for diagnostic technique. As relationships express themselves in inter-actions between the family members, the use of the joint interview suggests itself increasingly as an appropriate diagnostic technique. Individual discomfort, internal experiences, and personal feelings may require the person-to-person interview as the most appropriate channel

[1] Otto Pollak, 'Design of a Model of Healthy Family Relationships as a Basis for Evaluative Research', *Social Service Rev view*, Vol. XXXI, December 1957, 369-75.
[2] Otto Pollak, 'Family Situations and Child Development', *Children*, September-October, 1947, 172-73.

for diagnostic information. When the interaction between two persons becomes the focus of diagnostic inquiry, however, direct clinical observation becomes preferable in the interest of both reliability and interviewing economy

After an identification of its necessary premises, family diagnosis and family therapy will benefit from a definition of concepts. It seems helpful to define a relationship between two persons not only in emotional but also in functional terms. To say that a relationship is good and warm or negative and cold expresses an evaluation of tremendous importance for human living, but it leaves the basis for the evaluation unidentified. In that sense it may be helpful to define every relationship as the functioning of two persons as need-satisfiers for one another. Family relationships then designate the nature and the quality of the functioning of the members as resource persons for the needs of others. These needs change with the age of the members and also with the age of the family group as an interpersonal organization. Every family member as a person has a history of his own, but the family as a group also has a history of its own which does not fully coincide with the life-histories of its members. The life-histories of the parents have their origins in other families and the life-histories of the children will take place largely in families which they will form by marriages of their own.

In our culture the family is a self-creating and self-liquidating organization. Normally it consists of three sub systems which in their development are interlocking and compensatory—the spouse system, the parent-child system, and the sibling system. The needs met in this organization are partly maturational and partly developmental needs. The spouses have to learn to find their emancipation from their childhood ties to a degree which enables them to assume the role of parenthood. They have then to meet the dependency needs of their own children in order to make their growth possible. The closeness of the parent-child relationship requires a certain loosening of the interpersonal relationship between the spouses. But later on husband and wife have to find again in their own relationship compensation for the relationship loss which the emancipation of their children implies; and, finally, they have to prepare for a measure of independence from one another so as to be able to live out their lives after being widowed.

Siblings, on the other hand, have to provide one another first of all with the support that comes from plurality representation of their own generation within the family. They have to provide one another with the strength that comes from numbers. If they are not of the same sex they can provide one another also with an awareness of bisexuality in the sharing of the home which is freed from the overpowering framework of adulthood. An only child or siblings who are all of the same sex will experience a person of the other sex in the house only in the role of a father or a mother and will be dependent on relative strangers for the experience of bisexuality on their own generational level. However important the sibling relationship may be, ultimately it must be loosened in order to enable the children to go out and draw apart in order to start independent families of their own. In the long run, the parents and the children have to develop increasingly into independent adults, because dependency as a permanent personality expression can be tolerated only in cultures which commonly have three-generation families. The latter, of course, prevent non pathological loneliness at any phase of the life-cycle and, therefore, do not have to foster independence as a desirable personality characteristic of the individual, but they are incompatible with the social and geographical mobility of our culture. We shall have to return to these relationship phenomena later on in our discussion of the model.

Against this background, the following areas of diagnostic study have been found helpful, although by no means fully satisfactory:

Family structure. This is an inventory of family membership based on the recognition of the importance of family composition for performance of family functions. It must be evaluated on the basis of the completeness of personal resources which the American two-generation family can optimally provide. A basic model would comprise the presence of both spouses and siblings of both sexes who are not so far separated from one another by age as to prevent their feeling a unity of generation. Against the standard provided by this model, actual family structures can be found to have excess structure in the persons of grandparents, aunts, or uncles who claim resource functions in the family group which our conjugal family system does not recognize and cannot utilize. When, on the other hand, one parent is absent, or there is a single child, or children of only one sex, or children who are too far apart in age to present a generational unit clearly separated from the parents, we have a case of structural deficit.

Family functions. In the spouse system, the marriage partners meet the needs of each other through the performance of functions which can be described as emotional, sexual, economic, and ego-strengthening. There is first of all mutual assistance in the maintenance of emotional security on an adult level.[1] The new association of a man and a woman in a home of their own provides them with mutual relief from the feelings of loss and loneliness which usually accompany the separation of self from parental figures and the social and geographical separation from one's childhood family. The spouses give one another a feeling of biological and social completion which is recognized by them as well as by their associates. They give one another an opportunity for non pathological regression, the security of receiving tenderness and consideration, provision of care, and the experience of a spectrum of common interests.[1]

In the sexual sphere there is social permissibility of the experience, the coupling effect of more or less constant availability for the discharge of physiological tension, and the promise or realization of self-perpetuation.

In the economic sphere we have in our society a division of labour between the spouses as well as co-operation and interchangeability. The provision of income, although still expected to be the husband's function in many instances, can be shared or in an emergency taken over by the wife. In some instances the wife can undertake the function of the income provider also as an investment in the man's future by thus permitting him a quality and intensity of professional training that would be unattainable for him under a more traditional division of labour in the couple's economic activities. Utilization of income for the provision of consumer goods will be the primary function of the wife, although major purchase decisions will be made co-operatively as a rule. Practically unnoticed, the home created by the spouses is likely to be also the only area in which they will still experience tangible private property. In our corporate society, this is becoming more and more a unique function of the home in which one is husband or wife. Except for farmers and professional persons who work as private entrepreneurs, we earn our income with tools and equipment which we do not own and accumulate whatever financial competence we acquire in such intangible property rights as insurance benefits, pension rights, bonds, stocks, and bank deposits.

In the area of ego support and ego development the spouses, according to this model, aid one another in strengthening socially

---

[1] William J. Goode, 'The Sociology of the Family: Horizons in Family Theory', in *Sociology Today*, ed. Robert K. Merton, Leonard Broom and Leonard S. Cottrell, Jr., Basic Books, New York, 1959, p. 184.

[2] David Beres, M.D., 'The Person and the Group: Object Relationships', in *Psychoanalysis and Social Work*, ed. Marcel Heiman, M.D., International Universities Press, New York, 1953, p. 69.

adaptive mechanisms of defence. As far as autonomous ego functions are concerned, they help one another in the learning of spouse and parental roles and thus contribute to one another's adult socialization. Perhaps most important, they give each other freedom to express a measure of individuality which making a living in an industrial and bureaucratic society frequently does not permit. In this way they help one another in the development and maintenance of a feeling of adult identity.

In making a family diagnosis based on this model, attention will have to be paid to the performance of the following functions of the parent-child relationship. The parents promote the maturation of the children through physical and emotional nurture.[1] They help them to develop body-control skills[2] and primary interpersonal relationship skills in the process of socialization.[3] They provide anchor points for sexual identification,[4] prevent inversion,[5] provide the basis for super-ego formation,[6] and assist in the development of ego functioning.[7] They arrange and control the contact between the children and educational as well as play and health resources outside the family. The parents encourage emancipation in adolescents with the aim of helping them to achieve separate identities in adulthood and intermittently provide a refuge for them when, tired from the emotional strain of their ventures into separation and independence, the children seek a temporary retreat in dependency.

Minimal functions to be performed by the children themselves are seen in the achievement of a degree of biological and emotional maturation as well as intellectual and interactional development which will protect the parents against either social censure or pity from members of their own groups of reference.

In the sibling system brothers and sisters provide for one another, first of all, models of behaviour which can be imitated with relative ease because they are not so overwhelmingly superior as those re-

---

[1] Rene A. Spitz, M.D., 'Hospitalism', in *Psychoanalytic Study of the Child*, Vol. 1, International Universities Press, New York, 1945, pp. 53-74.
[2] Lawrence R. Frank, 'Cultural Control and Physiological Autonomy', in *Personality in Nature, Society, and Culture*, ed. Clyde Kluckhohn, Henry A. Murray and David M. Schneider; Alfred A. Knopf, New York, 1950, pp. 113-16.
[3] Erik H. Erikson, *Childhood and Society*, W. W. Norton & Co., New York, 1950, pp. 67-92.
[4] Sigmund Freud, *The Ego and the Id*, trans. Joan Riviere, Hogarth Press, London, 1927, p. 41.
[5] Sigmund Freud, *Three Contributions to the Theory of Sex*, Nervous and Mental Disease Publishing Co., New York, 1918, p. 88.
[6] Sigmund Freud, *The Ego and the Id*, op. cit., p. 39.
[7] Otto Pollak, 'Design of a Model of Healthy Family Relationships . . .', op. cit., p. 371.

presented by parents or teachers. This makes a relatively small age difference between siblings a helpful factor in the performance of a primary sibling function. Such a relatively manageable age difference also suggests to the younger child that maturation and development are in store for him in the near future. It permits him a displacement of oedipal feeling upon less threatening individuals than the parents. Related is the already mentioned function of siblings to provide for one another either directly or indirectly through friends the recognition of bisexuality on the level of their own generation. Most important, perhaps, the siblings help one another to learn adaptive mechanisms of sharing. Living in a family means in most instances the first encounter with the reality of material and emotional scarcity. In our model, siblings learn to share the resources of the family home for play space, work space, and sometimes even sleeping space. They learn to share the parental means available for financing recreation and education. Perhaps even more significant, they learn to share love and attention. Finally, they experience in their awareness of one another the benefits of becoming individuals and thus of establishing personal identity.

The family functions which the individual members are expected to perform for one another are usually conceptualized as social roles. We understand thereby the cultural expectation of the use of a person's capacities, predispositions, and environmental opportunities for the need satisfaction of others. These others in turn are expected to perform complementary social roles and thus satisfy the needs of the former. From this conceptual point of view, the family model can be visualized as a relatively constant interrelationship of role performances with individually and socially satisfactory results. Pervading the three sub systems is a functioning of the total system which provides the family members with a consciousness of group identity apart from all other groupings which they claim and which society accords to them.

Feelings and relationship tendencies. In our family diagnosis model the complementary role performance of the family members is evaluated in predominantly positive terms. This positive feeling tone exists in all three sub systems of the family. Ambivalence is recognized as unavoidable and utilized for the emotional preparation for necessary separations which precede, accompany, and follow the emancipation of an individual's self from his psychological ties to members of his family. Out of the experience of positive feelings for one another in interplay with the experience of negative feelings grow a number of

K

transactional processes which produce either a tendency towards increasing closeness or a tendency towards gradual emancipation.

These transactional processes are conceptualized as relationship tendencies and visualized as occurring in the following developmental framework: After marriage the spouses go through a period of increasingly more gratifying complementary role performance and correspondingly experience a tendency towards increasing interdependence and closeness. When children are born to them this closeness is somewhat relaxed, enabling the parents to meet the dependency and growth needs of the children. As these demands of child-rearing are felt, marital closeness takes on a different character. Although the ties between the spouses are increased, the demands of child care and child love require a certain loosening of their demands for purely interpersonal responses between themselves. As the demands of child care are met and parental love is responded to, closeness is growing in the parent-child relationship. When the oedipal phase has been lived through and the child's wishes for direct gratification of his libidinal impulses by his parents have been frustrated, this closeness in turn goes through a period of reduction, freeing the children for a constructive school experience and increasing toleration of separation from the parents also in other contexts. Accompanying the emancipation of the children in adolescence we find in the model a renewed increase of closeness in the marital relationship between the parents. This provides husband and wife with an emotional protection against the experience of loss through the separation of their adult children from them. Finally, as the difficulties of ageing make themselves felt, the unavoidable negative reactions to the deterioration of role-performance between the marriage partners create a certain basis for the tolerability of bereavement and widowhood.

Between siblings, strengthening of generational unity is overcoming sibling rivalry and leading to a positive experience of family relatedness which helps in the striving for identity and growth. As these developmental goals can be more and more independently pursued or at least pursued with help from age-mates who are not blood-related, these feelings are again relaxed, permitting the siblings the creation of geographically and socially separated lives in independent adulthood.

Against these feeling tone and relationship tendency standards, actual feeling experiences and relationship developments can be evaluated in terms of feeling disturbances and relationship arrests, reversals, or accelerations. Examples of such relationship tendency deviations can be easily recalled from professional practice. There are adults who even after marriage remain tied to their own parents and thus find themselves unable to establish interdependence with their spouses. There are persons who because of unresolved oedipal ties spend their lives in sham searches for appropriate mates. There are spouses who become increasingly separated from one another and turn to divorce. There are spouses who turn to the seeking of substitute gratifications in over-determined professional or civic activities and others who turn to marital unfaithfulness. Finally, there are young people who find themselves married at ages at which they should still experiment with emancipation and those who find themselves parents before they have had time to establish marital closeness.

The nature and reasons of family dynamics. Within this framework of study, family diagnosis becomes concerned with deviations from our conception of family health in terms of structure, functions (role performance), feelings, and relationship tendencies. This must not be construed, however, as an approach leading to exclusive localization of disturbance. It is likely that incompleteness of the family structure, such as the absence of a parent or lack of generational unity in the ages of the siblings, will affect all family relationships. Similarly, it can be expected that the disturbance of a spouse relationship will express itself in all parent-child relationships and consequently in the sibling relationships in the family. This tendency of one family-relationship disturbance to produce disturbances in other relationships within the family could be conceptualized as the principle of 'pervasiveness of family disturbance'. Localization of relationship disturbances or specifications, therefore, cannot be assumed in the study of family pathology without special evidence. It is, however, by no means impossible. The principle of 'indeterminacy in human development' may well be at work. This principle refers to the power of the human mind to react to experience in a creative and inventive rather than in an incorporating and imitating way. Consequently, human beings, although part of the same family, may react to the stimulus of family-relationship disturbance in ways which cannot be categorized as family-relationship disturbance. They may resist contagion and react to pathology with health. They may do so not only because of creativeness in human interaction but also because of the time at which they have to encounter the stimulus of relationship disturbance in the family. Disturbance of a family relationship may occur early in the history of a family or late as a result of death, illness, or unexpected pregnancy. The later it occurs in the family history the more fortified the individual members may be against its impact. Yet the principle of indeterminacy cannot be counted upon to operate. Such an operation would have to be investigated as a possible exception to the principle of pervasiveness of family disturbances.

If the family structure shows a deficit in normally available carriers of family roles, the principle of pervasiveness of family disturbance will probably express itself in a role redistribution within the family membership resulting in personality conflicts which are likely to accompany the assumption by an individual of roles incompatible to him. Thus siblings may be forced into roles of parent substitutes, children into roles properly belonging to spouses, and surviving parents into roles properly belonging to a parent of the other sex. In such instances, ego defences are likely to be disturbed and role performance to be inadequate. Structural deficits may lead not only to role redistributions but also to psychological fabrications of relationship loss which are unchecked by reality testing. The death of a family member, for example, may create an internal overestimation of what the deceased would have done for a family member, if he had been living. Thus he may provide an unrealistic frame of reference for the evaluation of what the substitute role-taker actually does.

When family structure is complete, role performance by family members may still be inadequate because of lack of readiness for role assumptions or change of roles required by the transition of the family group from one key period to another. But while, in incomplete family structures resulting from illness, bereavement, divorce, or desertion, role assumptions are likely to interfere with socially adaptive defences, relationship disturbances in complete families are likely to result from the interference of socially maladaptive defences with appropriately assigned roles or from the existence of incompatible defences in members of the family. The closer the maladaptive defence to the revelation of the id or superego impulse which it conceals or the greater the incompatability of defences, the greater the interference with appropriate role performance. Since role performance of one, however, in most instances influences the role performance of the partner in a family relationship, maladaptive defences in one probably will affect negatively not only role performance of the immature family members but also of those with whom he interacts in complementary role relationships. Similarly, mutual defence disturbance between the partners of a family relationship will probably also affect their role performance not only towards one another but also towards other members of the family. In consequence, the nature of family pathology can be usually described in identifying the location of the family group on the id-ego-superego continuum. When behaviour of parents seems to be largely id-determined, we will in all likelihood find dominance of id factors also in the behaviour of children. When a specific ego defence produces dysfunction in role performance between a parent and a child we are likely to find similar ego defence disturbances producing also dysfunctions in other role contexts within the family. Similarly, we are likely to find families in which the interactions and transactions among the members are all superego dominated with maladaptive consequences.

Having identified structural and functional deficiencies, completion of a family diagnosis requires recognition of predominant feeling tones and the resulting relationship disturbances with which the family members react to these deficiencies. As mentioned above, these can be reversals, arrests, or accelerations of relationship tendencies which healthy family development in our culture is expected to show.

A schema of family diagnosis based on these considerations would have to contain an identification of dysfunctions and of the resulting relationship tendency deviations among the family members. This account of family pathology would have to be explained in structural or dynamic terms or both. On that basis a treatment plan will have to be developed which would tend to bolster or relieve the family structure by the utilization of outside resources, to aid the family members in improving their role performance through the development of less mutually harmful expressions of their ego defences, or to work in both directions.

13

FAMILY DIAGNOSIS:
TRENDS IN THEORY AND PRACTICE*

M. ROBERT GOMBERG

In a review of the literature, one finds that it is only in the very recent past that there has been a concentration of conceptualization and practical illustrations of psychosocial diagnosis and family-centred treatment. Since about 1950 a number of rather important contributions have helped to clarify family orientation in diagnosis and treatment. The literature concentrates increasingly upon a holistic approach; one that recognizes the interdependence between individual diagnosis and family diagnosis, between socio-cultural factors and psychological factors, and between the treatment of the individual's failures in adjustment and adaptation and the treatment of the family.

References to Mary Richmond recur, not only in acknowledgment of her pioneering role in the formulation of theory and methods in the past, but in reassessing and reaffirming the value of many aspects of social diagnosis to present practice. She emphasized the importance of the family as a unit; the importance of cultural, social, and economic influences on family stability and adjustment; the importance of interpersonal relationships within the family matrix. Actually she anticipated such concepts as social role, family balance, and role reciprocity. Many writers have pointed out that in the course of our development beyond Miss Richmond we lost sight of some basic precepts of social diagnosis and treatment as we went through a crucial phase of our development—the incorporation into theory and practice of psychodynamics, of insight into the inner life of the individual. We do not need to understand here how urgently needed was the new psychological dimension to our understanding. If temporarily we lost contact with social phenomena, it was because there was such a critical need, in casework theory and practice, of an applied psychology. As

* Published in *Social Casework*, Vol. XXXIX, Nos. 2-3, February-March 1958.

frequently happens in a learning process, there is a tendency to forget
or put aside the old as we become preoccupied with the new.
Ultimately one achieves mastery of a subject through an integration
of all relevant knowledge.

If in the course of our development we 'strayed', as Frances Scherz
has put it,[1] and for periods of time lost sight of the family as a unit as
well as some other sound precepts of theory and practice, in order to
learn, incorporate and integrate a knowledge of psychodynamics, of
emotional phenomena, then it is equally important for us to examine
the reasons for our return to a concern with the total family, with social
factors, and so on. I believe that it is because, after a most productive
and rewarding learning experience, we began to feel the limitations
implicit in a sole reliance on an individualized psychology. Existing
clinical diagnostic tools and classifications focus exclusively on individual personality. Our attempt in casework to encompass the larger
whole, to include the social factors and the family in our diagnosis, is
only partially successful. No diagnostic or conceptual system exists
which describes, assesses, or classifies the family configuration, yet
this is clearly needed if the diagnosis of the individual is not to be in a
vacuum but rather within the context of the social and emotional
environment in which he lives, adjusts, suffers, fails, or succeeds. We
must not choose between a concept of the family and a psychology of
the individual; it is through a balanced understanding of the inter-
relatedness between the two that we can achieve the most meaningful
understanding and the most effective treatment. An understanding of
the individual as an individual is incomplete unless we can have a
comprehensive understanding of the family of which he is a part. The
understanding of the family is incomplete unless we have some comprehension of the separate individuals that comprise the family. The
individual is part of the family; the family is part of the individual. We
do not choose between individual and family; we do not choose between inner and outer forces, but rather must develop a comprehensive
frame of reference that helps us to understand and to weigh all these
phenomena in relation to each other.

The present writer, dealing with somewhat the same theme, wrote
the following:
'Diagnosis achieves an extra dimension in family-centred treatment.
It offers both a vertical (etiological) and horizontal (current interaction) perspective in studying a personality or intra-familial conflict

[1] Frances H. Scherz, 'What is Family-Centered Casework?', *Social Casework*, Vol.
XXXIV, No. 8, 1953, pp. 343-349.

and it inevitably influences the treatment process. In addition to evaluating the developmental forces which have influenced the shaping of the personality of the client—child or adult—equal attention is paid to the current family Gestalt.'[1]

Dr Otto Pollak[2] also wrote on this same theme of the family as a unit, emphasizing the social interactional character of the family, the chain of interdependence of individual behaviour, and the influence of the treatment of one individual on others in the family. He too called attention to the critical lack of a diagnostic and conceptual system which hampers family diagnosis and treatment:

'The explanation seems to lie . . . in a lack of necessary conceptual equipment for taking these factors into account. Phenomena for which technological terminology is not available to the practitioner tend to remain unconsidered.'[3]

This thinking underscores the fact that our conceptualization has been primarily in relation to *individual* personality, growth, adjustment, pathology, and so on. All of us are aware that in our practice we have worked with families, have planned with and for them, and were helpful to them. Yet there is no doubt but that our diagnostic formulations, our theory, have been framed in terms only of the individual, and lacked any crystallized, conceptual system of family dynamics and family interaction, which dealt with the family as a unitary organism.

In 1953 Dr Irene Josselyn made a valuable contribution to this subject:

'This description of psychological development (of the individual) does not touch upon the meaning of the family unit but only upon the meaning of the individual family members to a particular person . . . The family can be defined politically, economically, and sociologically. It needs also to be studied psychologically. Not the individual but the family is the smallest unit of our social structure. The family can be analysed by studying its individual parts, but the findings must be synthesized before it can be understood as a unit . . . The neuroses and psychoses of the unit rather than the neuroses and psychoses of its component parts can then be understood. By studying family pathology we can determine what constitutes family health.'[4]

[1] M. Robert Gomberg, 'Trends Toward Family-Oriented Treatment in Social Casework', *Jewish Social Service Quarterly*, Vol. XXX, No. 3, 1954, p. 256.

[2] Otto Pollak, and others, *Social Science and Psychotherapy for Children*, Russell Sage Foundation, New York, 1952.

[3] Otto Pollak, 'Relationship between Social Science and Child Guidance Practice', *American Sociological Review*, Vol. XVI, No. 1, 1951, p. 63.

[4] Irene M. Josselyn, M.D., 'The Family as a Psychological Unit', *Social Casework*, Vol. XXXIV, No. 8, 1953, pp. 336-43.

In this excellent article there is a reaffirmation of the essential basic principles of individual growth and development, a pointing to the essential need for a psychology of the family, for descriptions and classifications of a family typology of normal family development and family pathology. But then Dr Josselyn underscores the fact that we are far from having achieved a defined understanding of the psychological nature of the family entity. Dr John P. Spiegel, who, along with Dr Kluckhohn, is engaged in invaluable pioneering research in a related, vital area of interest, underscores the limitations of individual psychological definition and description, and affirms a fully developed understanding of the psychology of the family as a necessary goal towards which to strive:

'A constant observer of the family—or of any other persistent group process—has a(n) . . . impression that much of what occurs in the way of behaviour is not under the control of any one person or even a set of persons, but rather the upshot of complicated processes beyond the ken of anyone involved. Something in the group process itself takes over as a steering mechanism and brings about results which no one anticipates, or wants, whether consciously or unconsciously. Or the steering mechanism may bring about a completely unexpected pleasant effect. On the basis of numerous observations, we were struck with the fact that so often what is functional for one member of the family group may be dysfunctional for the family as a whole. The opposite also holds: What is functional for the family as a whole may have very harmful effects on one person. These phenomena take place unwittingly, not only because of the unconscious dynamics within each person, but also because of the operation of the system of relation in which the members of the family are involved.'[1]

Throughout all these papers the need for identifying, describing, and classifying 'family personality' as an entity is affirmed.

What are the implications of what we have reported thus far? There is always the danger, when we isolate an area for further research and investigation, of devaluing what we know, of becoming overly uncertain and cautious about existing theory and methods. The converse of this is that too frequently the advocates of a new finding, a new hypothesis, in order to make it felt, known, and accepted, tend to overstate its case, and instead of letting it find its appropriate place within an enlarged frame of reference they proceed to set up shop with a new

---

[1] John P. Spiegel, M.D., 'The Resolution of the Role Conflict within the Family', *Psychiatry: Journal for the Study of Interpersonal Processes*, Vol. XX, No. 1, 1957, pp. 1-16.

'school of thought'. What the field of human relations requires least in our present stage of development is additional 'schools of thought'. In psychiatry and psychoanalysis, psychology, sociology, and casework, the urgent need is for research, tolerance, and open mindedness towards ultimate development and validation of an integrated conceptual system about man and society. The fact that the writings to which I have referred point sharply to the need for a new level of study and understanding about family dynamics does not for a moment overshadow the tremendous growth and achievement in that very direction over the last years. On two levels, practice and research, there has been persistent and remarkable advance. On the level of practice and experience, the very fact that the need for a psychology of the family as a unit has emerged has brought about one of the most creative and imaginative periods in our practice. Our technical literature bespeaks a vitality and excitement and demonstration. It would be an impossible task within a single paper to abstract or highlight the many contributions. The trends, however, are marked.

From psychosocial studies and diagnosis of the family and from analysis of treatment goals and methods are emerging the data and the experience which inevitably will provide us with the knowledge of family dynamics which we seek. More and more discussions appear of complementarity, role reciprocity, the 'fit' of relationships. Knowledge of individual psychosocial dynamics is now being adapted to use in comprehending the nature of family equilibrium, social roles, and role expectations characteristic between husband and wife, parent and child, siblings, and within the family group as a whole. Increasingly apparent are such questions as: What factors, internal or external, produce the kind of stress that disturbs the level of functioning? To what extent was the degree of family balance that was achieved based upon a flexible, fluid, adaptable complementarity, and to what degree was it dependent upon a rigid, and therefore vulnerable, combination of personality needs?

Treatment goals are more frequently stated as bifocal: help to the individual with his problems in adaptation, but help to the individual within the context of helping the family achieve that level of balance, equilibrium, and functioning that seems appropriate to it and, therefore, seems most likely to offer the kind of emotional configuration within which the individual adaptation is likely to take place and be sustained. Although individuals are viewed separately and may be treated separately, a concern for the level of family functioning is developing.

In the literature, it is of special interest to note how this newer interest cuts across all functional fields. Although different settings have special problems and require special knowledge and skill, the overall conception of psychosocial diagnosis and family-centred treatment is generically intriguing. Such an orientation is held in common by writers on otherwise diverse subject matter: Max Siporin in 'Family-Centred Casework in a Psychiatric Setting',[1] S. N. Sherman in 'Group Counselling',[2] M. R. Gomberg in 'Family-Oriented Treatment of Marital Problems',[3] and Mrs Scherz in her article on 'Direct Treatment of Children in a Family Agency'.[4]

One could continue with various illustrations from the fields of child placement, the therapeutic day nursery, group work, and so on, all tending in the direction of viewing the family as a psychosocial unitary organism. The orientation towards the family cuts across different professional fields and disciplines: casework, psychiatry, psychology, sociology, social science—even physical medicine. It is clear then that what we are dealing with is an expanded understanding of human behaviour and the many and complex forces that influence it.

We mentioned earlier that two developments in recent years are indications of progress in conceptualization. The first, already commented on, had to do with developments in practice and in accompanying conceptualization of family diagnosis and family treatment. The second stimulating development in recent years has been the blossoming of research efforts in social work in collaboration with the social sciences. Our profession always has taken a high degree of responsibility for self-study and for self-evaluation; these, however, are significantly different from technically designed research conducted by a team of trained research personnel and casework staff. In the past we had a relatively distant relationship to the fields of sociology, anthropology, social psychology, and many of the social and behavioural sciences. They represented 'resource material' but rarely made effective penetration into our thinking and practice. Casework itself is now turning to scientific and disciplined research; together with psychiatry it is also eagerly closing the wide gap which had separated it from developments in the social sciences. A publication

[1] Max Siporin, 'Family-Centred Casework in a Psychiatric Setting', *Social Casework*, Vol. XXXVII, No. 4, 1956, pp. 167-74.
[2] Sanford N. Sherman, 'Group Counseling', in *Neurotic Interaction in Marriage*, Victor W. Eisenstein, M.D. (ed.), Basic Books, New York, 1956, pp. 296-302.
[3] M. Robert Gomberg, 'Family-Oriented Treatment of Marital Problems', *Social Casework*, Vol. XXXVII, No. 1, 1956, pp. 3-10.
[4] Frances H. Scherz, 'Direct Treatment of Children in a Family Agency', *Social Casework*, Vol. XXXIX, No. 2-3, February-March 1958.

specifically related to our area of interest—family diagnosis—is the report of Community Research Associates, *Classification of Disorganized Families for Use in Family Oriented Diagnosis and Treatment*.[1] Significant contributions from the field of social science have been made by John P. Spiegel and Florence Kluckhohn in their Harvard project, by Nathan W. Ackerman in his work on family diagnosis, and by Parsons and Bales, Clyde Kluckhohn, Foote and Cottrell, Reuben Hill, and many others. The Research Institute on Family Relations of the Jewish Family Service of New York and the Russell Sage Foundation currently are working together on a research project in the area of family diagnosis, interaction, classification, and so on.

In the process of rapprochment between social science and the disciplines, such as casework and psychiatry, which are based on dynamic psychology, it is noteworthy how interpenetration of ideas is occurring. One of many examples of the penetration of social science in casework appears in Helen Harris Perlman's excellent book, *Social Casework: A Problem-Solving Process*. In her chapter on 'The Person', a discussion of personality and the range and variety of factors, constitutional, psychological, social, and cultural that join in the influencing of any personality, she writes:
'A person at any stage of his life not only is "a product" of nature and nurture but is also and always "in process" of being in the present and becoming in the future . . . the person's "being and becoming behaviour" is both shaped and judged by the expectations he and his culture have invested in the status and the major social roles he carries.'[2]

Mrs Perlman goes on to develop the significance of role theory and the part that it plays in understanding personality structure.

Much current research and writing in sociology include an interest not only in social process but in psychological processes, in psychodynamics. Thus, for example, in Foote and Cottrell,[3] and in Parsons and Bales,[4] the conceptualizations include levels of consideration of psychological motivations as well as interactive sociocultural factors that influence behaviour. Conversely, in the articles quoted earlier from the literature of both casework and psychiatry, one notes the penetration of concepts of social process. There is an increasing

[1] Community Research Associates, *Classification of Disorganised Families for use in Family Oriented Diagnosis and Treatment*, New York, 1954.
[2] Helen Harris Perlman, *Social Casework: A Problem-Solving Process*, University of Chicago Press, Chicago, 1957, p. 19.
[3] Nelson N. Foote and Leonard S. Cottrell, Jr., *Identity and Inter Personal Competence*, University of Chicago Press, Chicago, 1955.
[4] Talcott Parsons and Robert F. Bales, *Family, Socialization and Interaction Process*, The Free Press, Glencoe, Ill., 1955.

interpretation that is on the road to what Grinker called a 'unified theory of human behaviour'.[1]

The developments in interpenetration and integration of the differing disciplines although offering promise of an expanded comprehension of the family Gestalt, require a note of caution. Concepts of role, organization, small group theory, and culture value orientation are complex in themselves. To integrate them with dynamic psychological—and psychobiological—concepts is a formidable task. It will take thoughtfulness, time, experiment, and many refinements and reformulations.

A second caution: We must not confuse the expansiveness in our psychosocial view of the total family, our *efforts* to understand the interactions and the interdependence between individual and family diagnosis, with actually having *arrived* at a crystallized conceptual system or a classification of family typologies. Each of the writers reported earlier, particularly Spiegel and Josselyn, hypothesized some core superordinate entity in discussing the family as a unit. Dr Spiegel said that something in the 'Group process itself takes over as a steering mechanism and brings about results which no one anticipates . . .'[2] Dr Josselyn wrote. 'If the family unit is anthropomorphized, . . . the neuroses and psychoses of the unit rather than the neuroses and psychoses of its component parts can then be understood . . .'[3] Having moved forward a great deal in our family orientation and conceptualization, we must not delude ourselves that we have 'arrived'. We must remain scientifically open-minded, experimental, and critical. We must strenuously prevent any rigidities from setting in and avoid 'validating' through repetition rather than research and empirical testing.

Particularly in the treatment of children is the need apparent for a theory that conceptualizes the whole family and a method of treatment that encompasses the whole family. Dr Sidney Green has pointed out that both in the case of the normal child, and obviously more emphatically in the case of the disturbed child, the personality of the child is almost organically interwoven with those of the parents and other significant members of the family. The disturbed, and therefore more immature child, is relatively more inextricably bound with parents who are usually themselves conflicted and 'pathogenetic'. The

[1] Roy R. Grinker (ed.), *Toward a Unified Theory of Human Behaviour*, Basic Books, New York, 1956.
[2] John P. Spiegel, M.D., 'The Resolution of the Role Conflict within the Family', *Psychiatry: Journal for the Study of Interpersonal Processes*, Vol. XX, No. 1, 1957, pp. 1-16.
[3] Irene M. Josselyn, M.D., 'The Family as a Psychological Unit', *Social Casework*, Vol. XXXIV, No. 8, 1953, pp. 336-43.

family 'transactional field', its stability and integrational potential, will be a larger determinant of whether the child moves towards further maturity and autonomy or towards character or personality deviations. This fact adds emphasis to the need to view the triangular relationship as a dynamic entity—both diagnostically and therapeutically.

Dr Nathan Ackerman, who has made major contributions to the concept of family diagnosis and treatment, recently wrote: 'Family diagnosis seeks a means for identifying the family as a psychological entity in and out of itself, a way of assessing its psychosocial configuration and mental health functioning, a basis of classification and differential diagnosis of family types, and finally a method of correlating the dynamics of individual and family behaviour. The ultimate goal is a social psychopathology of family life . . . In such an undertaking the dimensions of diagnostic thinking are expanded beyond the limits of the internal economy of personality so as to embrace three interrelated sets of processes: what goes on inside the individual; what goes on between this individual and other significant family members; and the psychosocial patterns of the family as a whole. We seek here to correlate the emotional balance within the individual with the balance of role adaptation in family pairs and this, in turn, with the emotional balance of the family group itself.'[1]

Dr Ackerman proposes a systematic approach, 'a practical scheme' for correlating the many different levels and criteria for making a family diagnosis. He suggests defining (1) the self-image or psychological identity; (2) homeostasis; (3) the adaptation to family role, new experience, reality testing, and so on for (a) each individual in the family, (b) important family pairs or triads, and (c) the family as a whole; and (4) pathogenic conflicts, symptoms, and corresponding restitution mechanisms.

The point of view developed so far in this paper can be further specified and concretized by reference to selected aspects of a case. In some representative extrapolations from this case we will utilize parts of Dr Ackerman's schematic formula as one practical approach.

The Gray family came to us at a point of serious distress. Twelve-year-old Albert, the younger of two boys, had begun quite suddenly to resist going to school. Such provocative behaviour was new for him and unexpected and acutely distressing to the family. The family had just moved to a new suburban community, and after attending

---

[1] Dr. Nathan Ackerman, 'The Role of the Family in Diagnostic Process', paper presented at the 33rd Annual Meeting of the American Orthopsychiatric Association, New York, 1956.

school for about two and a half months Albert refused to return. For the past month he had insisted that he was unable to attend. The family tried everything—persuasion, bribery, punishment, and physical coercion—only to find all of these approaches aggravating the problem, the boy becoming more distressed, panicky, and insistent on his inability to return to school.

The mother and father, at their request, were seen jointly the first few times. Background information and the perceptions of the parents as individuals and as a pair must perforce be telescoped. Mr G, thirty-seven, was young-looking, well-dressed, of good intelligence, well-spoken, with a great deal of vitality. He took the lead in describing the situation. At times Mrs G made relevant contributions; at other times she fussed with minor details. One noted immediately her gratification in being precise and accurate, and her need to keep 'the record' in order. Later, this trait became clear as a component in her personality and in their relationship. Their surprise and near-belief as well as disappointment in Albert's behaviour, as contrasted with his older brother's, studded their description. Such behaviour seemed beyond their cultural ken.

Mr G was an aggressive, driving man—the archtype of the 'self-made' man whose badge of success was his business and his family. His business career was a personal triumph of single-minded, even ruthless, perseverance and inventiveness. From an office 'in his hat' he had created a plant employing several hundred people. His family was built with an almost parallel pride in his own genius. His aggressive adaptive pattern was honed* in a struggle for his autonomy with a dominating, destructive mother, and also out of a reaction formation to identification with a weak, ineffectual, passive father. Mr G was partly sympathetic to, partly contemptuous of, a younger sister who had succumbed to the overpowering mother.

Mrs G was bright, personable, but subject to a constant brooding sense of inadequacy. Her formal education was far beyond her husband's, including a Master's degree in education. She had a hostile, dependent relationship to her mother, who was extremely attractive and highly intellectual, and who, through disdain and cruel manipulative wit, dominated her home.

Mrs G, never fully separated from her mother, had an incompletely realized female identity; she repressed rebellion and competition with her mother, and became the overly good, conforming daughter. Mrs G, too, had a sibling, a brother three years her junior. Her

* Sharpened.

brother, although favoured by the mother, apparently had floundered
through life, was weak, dependent, and ineffective. Mrs G had an
affectionate, protective concern for her brother but also felt him to
be hopeless and futile. A sister transference to Albert was obvious.

Mrs G had a rather complaining, whining demeanour, although
she smiled continuously. She was extremely well organized and
efficient. She had never used her training in the educational field but
instead took a secretarial position in which she was highly competent.

The G's knew each other about a year prior to marriage. They were
both twenty-three when they married. Mr G was impressed with his
wife's education and was completely taken by this quiet, passive,
retiring, self-effacing personality. She was the antithesis of his mother
and he saw her as the 'ideal mate'. To Mrs G, Mr G's forcefulness,
aggressiveness, and sureness were most appealing. Here was a man
who could serve as armour against her mother's dominance and to
whom she could readily transfer her dependency. The other side of
the coin was that although Mrs G was in part free of her mother's
domination, her husband's forcefulness not only met some of her
dependency needs but tyrannized her with demands. Only well after
marriage did Mr G have to contend with her hypochondriacal complaints, her whinings, and her self-pitying efforts at manipulation. In
spite of these residual neurotic trends carried over from their respective
parental homes, the couple met so many of each other's needs, that
they were able to keep under good control the mutual resentments
and disappointments, and both found some measure of gratification
in their relationship.

It is interesting to note here that the level of complementarity that
was achieved is best described by Dr Spiegel's use of the term 'role
induction', that is, the decision-making in most of their interests and
activities was more or less unilaterally the husband's and reflected his
interests. Although the wife may have attempted to retain some
mastery through manipulation, by and large she was overpowered and
yielded. Her participation in these interests and activities afforded
some enjoyment and gratification but also expressed some of her
shallowness and preoccupation with detail rather than the wholeness
of experience. She remained partially uncommitted, on the periphery
of the activity, carrying the responsibilities for details which she always
enjoyed, whether they had to do with business or with social life.
Typically there was only one area apparent in which she had her way
and overcame her husband's preference. She had coerced him into
allowing her to continue active participation in the business. Her near-

FAMILY DIAGNOSIS   161

parasitic need to be with and part of him drove her into a stubborn, unrelenting insistence on her participation. Role induction contrasts with role modification, where there is some real feeling and sensitivity to the other person and his needs, and there is an evolution of patterns of mutual adaptation. Role modification was only marginally present in this marriage.

Both parents described the older son as having been 'easy', self-sufficient, and almost more of a friend than a child for as long as they could remember. Albert, on the other hand, from the very beginning, seemed to have more needs, more demands for attention. Although they were able in some part to meet these needs, they evinced a mild resentment for this intrusion upon their primary preoccupations with themselves, with each other, and with the business. The resentment was accompanied by sincere affection, pleasure, and pride in Albert as well as in his brother. Important, too, was their support of the children as favourites of the grandparents. They were envied by many members of the extended family.

Mr G's business had prospered and grown through the war years and the subsequent period. Previously the entire business was humble in size and conducted in their own home. Thus, Albert was used to having mother, father and brother in the home almost all the time. When he started school, the older brother took him to and from school, since they attended the same school. Several years prior to the family's move to the suburbs, the business had moved 'downtown'. Mr and Mrs G reported a great deal of conflict between them at the time the office was moved. Mrs G asserted her desire to work in the office, and Mr G opposed this strenuously, but for once his typical pattern of persuasion failed and he finally yielded. He said that later he was grateful that he had yielded because he could never get a book-keeper or secretary from the 'market' as competent or as responsible as his wife. In typical fashion, he thus re-established his hegemony even here in the area where he had clearly been coerced. When they moved to the new community, Albert felt deserted by his entire family. His mother and father would leave early, before he went to school, and they would return late in the evening. His older brother now attended high school and Albert had to go to a new school by himself. In addition, all his old peer associations were arbitrarily disrupted and he felt himself completely isolated and alone.

The parents described Albert as a very bright, attractive youngster who was small for his age. He was gifted with an IQ of 155. Other children were fond of him but they always treated him as the youngest

L

or 'baby' of the group. He was active in school, highly successful, and liked by his teachers. Although he could never reach authoritative positions like class officer or monitor, he was given other kinds of recognition that made school, by and large, a pleasurable experience for him. His parents were proud of his high intelligence and school success but annoyed about his small stature and his dependency needs. Albert's ego development was uneven—adequate in many areas but poor in the area of interpersonal relations with both adults and peers because of his immaturity, passivity, and dependency needs. These needs rarely alienated the other person but elicited protection and affectional responses. In his relationship with his mother there was latent conflict between the dependency needs of both, which, however, was in good part contained by the mother as a result of her gratifications in performing and conforming to her self-image as competent and efficient in all areas, including mothering; the child's defence against his father's demands and aggressiveness was to de-personalize the relationship and be 'performance-oriented' in school and other activities.

Albert was seen once at home. Then the parents were seen jointly four times in the office. The mother was being seen individually as well. After the parents had been seen for the fourth time, contact was established with Albert in the office. He was brought by his mother and later was able to travel by himself. The boy was seen for a period of eighteen months. The mother was seen weekly during this time; the mother and father jointly once every five or six weeks throughout the entire treatment. In addition there were three home visits with the entire family present and participating, and twice the father and Albert were seen together. Kenneth, the older boy, was seen twice by himself.

The first effort in working with the parents was to help them restore the marital equilibrium which had been disturbed by the youngster's difficulties. Their sense of futility in dealing with Albert had begun to lead them to recriminations against each other. Although there was concern and sympathy for the boy, at the same time there was a great deal of resentment and hostility, and both the parents identified the child with their own inadequate siblings. To bring the boy back to school the father had tried coercion and punishment, the mother had tried persuasion, and both had attempted to use Kenneth as a lever. When none of their devices worked, they began to blame each other.

In the course of the joint interviews each was critical of the other. Mrs G complained that her husband was too domineering and he complained that whenever there was a problem she simply began to whine and wait for him to take care of it. It was possible to help them ventilate these feelings, yet begin to see how each sought and brought out these very qualities in the other. There was productive discussion of how they used each other, where such use was essentially good and where it was destructive. Their patterns of helping and supporting each other in their own unique ways was identified, described, and supported. The very self-consciousness that was initiated by this discussion of their respective roles, their use and expectation of each other, seemed to reduce some of the rigidity of their patterns, and make each of them a little more aware of the other's feelings and needs.

In the course of the discussion with both parents, what became clear was that their overall urgency to get Albert back to school was so much more apparent than love or concern for him, that they had intensified his phobic defence. Each of them could identify the extent to which he or she had contributed to this situation.

In interviews with Mrs G alone, it was possible to work towards some degree of further understanding. She volunteered that she should have stayed at home with the boy; she just couldn't, and thus she could empathize with him in his fearfulness about going to school. She felt just as 'unreasonably fearful' of giving up work (home phobia). She talked of her relationship with her mother and how this had contributed to her low self-esteem. She could locate some of her motives for needing to be in business constantly with her husband. Her fear was that he would close the circle of his life around business, acquaintances, and possibly even other women, and have little or no need for her. Thus, by becoming both indispensable in the business and, at the same time, constantly in a position to watch him, she was attempting to protect herself against this fear. Over a period of time the interrelations between those attitudes and feelings in her parental home and her present family were clarified, the positive values she found in working were supported, and she was helped to move towards a part-time association with the business.

Once the husband was able to discharge some of his hostility and his resentment, he began to attack the child's problem with some of the same vigour with which he had previously attacked the child. He became interested in building a closer relationship with Albert, and although much of his effort was aggressively overdetermined, it was nonetheless rewarding both to him and to the boy. He began giving Albert considerably more of his time and interest.

Over the year and a half there was an increasing number of instances in which Mr G deferred to Mrs G's wishes and, of course, created some embarrassment for her as she began, after these many years, to take a modest role in making decisions for the family. Although the essential pattern remained the same, they developed some additional flexibility in their respective roles and expectations of each other.

Similar adaptations were taking place in the other relationships in the family. At a point in treatment where Albert and his father were being seen together in a joint interview, Albert brought into the open a feeling he had previously shared with the worker alone. Albert commented that he loved his father very much, thought he was a great guy, but was a little scared of him. Mr G was rather taken aback and after an unsuccessful effort to interrogate Albert as to what he had to be scared of, he noted that not infrequently people had felt this way towards him. Then, turning to Albert, he said he was sorry. It had been upsetting for him to hear this comment, and, strangely enough, Albert had now made him a little afraid of himself, because he really did not want to be that kind of person. While Albert's lip quivered and he was a little apologetic and surprised at himself for having been able to affect his father so, they physically moved towards each other in the room and it was evident that in spite of the awkwardness between them, they felt a little closer together.

After a year of treatment the entire family gathered with the worker for the second home visit. The atmosphere was generally warm and supportive to Albert. The father was working too hard in 'selling' the progress they had made, but he was really concerned and trying to be helpful. Although the mother's role was seasoned with little thrusts of self-pity, she seemed much more related than before to the feeling of the others. It was interesting to note that there was increased warmth flowing from and to the parents. The parents spoke with great pride about the boys' scholastic achievements, about Kenneth's athletic ability, his leadership in school, and about Albert's musical talent.

When they got to discussing the reasons for Albert's upsetting experience with school, he was the first to remind everybody that he had been back in school for some time and was doing well. Quite clearly and simply he indicated that he had been frightened when the family moved to the suburbs where he had no friends in the community or at school; that with Kenneth's going to another school and the house being empty, he had a feeling of loneliness that he just could not do anything about. He could not get himself to go to school although he knew that the family would be gathering in the evening.

With pride he reported that he now had a number of friends, was successful in school, and so on.

Kenneth, while agreeing with everything that Albert had said, made a telling observation. He said it seemed as though everybody, particularly the parents, was on a merry-go-round. He accused them of having been too busy; it didn't matter with what. They were always rushing to work or rushing to meetings. Although he knew that they loved the boys, they seemed to have no time to be with the family. They had to 'sneak' their family life in between more important events. He for one could not see why these other things were so important. Albert, who was feeling his oats, turned on his father and said, 'Sure. How many suits can you wear at one time? How many cars can you drive? You know you can't take it with you!'

It was interesting to note that the parents, although a little uneasy, nonetheless took this in their stride. The father acknowledged that sometimes his 'inside motor' ran him, and he just kept running, but this experience had helped him to get a sense of values. Although there was obviously hostile components in the thoughts the boys were expressing, these were not dominant. At this point they were describing a feeling of contrast of 'before and after', with some genuine sense of family identity having been achieved. It was not the boys pitted against the parents so much as their insistence on more time and space within the lives of their parents. If the father was a little embarrassed by all this, he nonetheless glowed with pride because he admired this forcefulness on the part of the boys. When the worker was leaving, Mr G made the observation that he guessed there were no 'doormats' in his family.

I have not reported this case chronologically or reported the process all the way through. Rather I have chosen to emphasize highlights of working with pairs or the joint group. As can be expected in a situation like this, Albert returned to school in a relatively short period of time. Mrs G, after the first number of joint and individual interviews, was helped to stay home for six weeks, doing some office work there. After Albert seemed more comfortable and ready to return to school, she settled into a part-time job. She could enjoy work more since she asked less of it. She took greater pride and gratification in her role as mother and home-maker. Albert was confirmed in the course of treatment. His superior confirmation speech and his conduct throughout the ceremony brought him attention and admiration from his own family and the extended family, with a symbolic and salutary effect upon his growth.

At the termination of treatment, the family had established a sounder equilibrium, with some increase in their own competence to understand and deal more adequately with each other's needs. It was hoped their capacity to cope with subsequent stress, intra-familial or external, would thereby be strengthened.

Here then is an illustration of how the personalities of two parents, forged in earlier life experience, both having uneven ego development and mixtures of healthy and neurotic needs and defences, combine into a marital pair and evolve a pattern of complementarity. We are dealing with relatively strong personality organization. The older child was absorbed into the family without undue stress, and the equilibrium was not disturbed, although one wonders about the impact on the child of his adaptation to the parental configuration and accommodation to their expectation. Nonetheless, he seemed to function well, and to show no sign of impaired development. The younger child's needs put some strain on the balance, but equilibrium was maintained until a combination of precipitants upset it. Even the choice of symptom by the boy had secondary values in hitting at an area where the parents' social and psychological values made them vulnerable. The parents at first tried strenuously to maintain the existing pattern. As they failed to resolve the particular crisis, a process of disorganization began to set in. The compensating features in the marital relationship began to fail and the neurotic features in both individuals came into greater prominence. The child's need for support, identity (personal and family), and family nurturing made him forgo the gratifications from performing at the level of mastery he had achieved in his own process of ego development, and regress. The family's search for outside help was an effort at 're-equilibration'.

I suggested in the introduction to this paper that one of the risks in describing and evaluating a new hypothesis is that at first it seems to overshadow or displace everything that came before. Family-centred diagnosis is, however, a logical extension in theory and practice of individually-oriented diagnosis and treatment.

Thus, in the G case, in the detailed working through of problems, much is similar to our past experience—the diagnostic appraisal of the separate personalities, the assessment of ego development and functioning. The delineation and evaluation of the defences, the decision as to supportive help for existing adaptive patterns, as against decisions to work towards modification of defences—all of these diagnostic and treatment considerations in working with members of this family, particularly the mother and one son, would reflect much of the practice with which we are familiar.

When we suggest 'anthropomorphizing' the family, we are obviously using a symbol for stressing the urgency of conceptualization of the family as an entity. In the further development of the concept and of working hypotheses, we assume that the dynamics and structure of the interactive process are different from that of individual personality. Individual and interactive phenomena influence each other and they overlap, but they must be viewed separately in order to determine how they affect each other. For a long time we have been aware that the psychic structure of the individual is motivational in interpersonal relationships. We had less clarity about the feed-back process. Complementarity in significant pair relationships and equilibrium in total family relations are group processes which influence, sometimes decisively, the adequacy of an individual's functioning or psychological development. Thus, a constructive combination may compensate individual neurotic tendencies, achieving not only a good balance between two or more family members, but aiding maturation and growth within the individual member.

If group processes have characteristics of their own, if the family Gestalt has a 'steering mechanism', how does one locate and attempt to influence it? Of course research will have to help determine whether or not there is such an entity, but empirically, observation seems to confirm this hypothesis.

In the case illustration I have attempted to point to one experimental approach to the study and treatment of the interaction; that is, to incorporate joint interviews with significant pairs or groups within the family—husband-wife, father-son, mother-son, and total family— into the treatment process. Such joint interviewing serves to expand diagnostic understanding through direct observation of behaviour and interpersonal processes in action. No description by one member can communicate significant nuances in relationship as effectively as direct observation. In addition to its diagnostic value, the joint interview offers additional opportunity for treatment of special areas of conflict unique to the particular combination.

The primary needs defined in the beginning of the paper—research that will lead to classification of family typologies, practice that will strengthen differential family diagnosis, and treatment methodology that encompasses individual and interactive processes—will not be met quickly. Long and patient effort, creative and courageous experiment, and tolerance for new ideas seasoned with a healthy scepticism will be required.

14

APPLYING FAMILY DIAGNOSIS
IN PRACTICE*

HENRY FREEMAN

THE original intent was that this paper might describe seasoned practice in the use of family diagnosis in a family casework agency. At the outset it must be understood that our experience falls far short of such a scope. However, we are making an attempt to understand what a family diagnosis truly should be, how it may be best applied in a family agency, and, finally, what needs to be added to the present skill of the professional staff. At this point in our experience, we find that the approach described here essentially adds to the already firmly established diagnostic disciplines found in family casework. This approach, which gives a broader perspective on the function and dysfunction of an individual, is particularly helpful in clarifying the positive functioning of any individual in the family unit. We anticipate that further experience will add to and perhaps modify our skills in helping clients.

In the following three areas we have identified some of the things that we believe need elaboration in order to achieve a family diagnosis that has meaning in practice. We need:

1. A review of the deeply ingrained professional focus on the individual's personal development and experiences exclusively in order to see individual development in the perspective of the family as an entity.
2. Application of specific knowledge based on the combination of our own experience and material from related disciplines on the structure, dynamics, and functions of the family as an entity.
3. Adaptation of already established disciplined skills in exploration and evaluation to the understanding of how 'the family' is getting

* Published in *The Social Service Review*, Vol. XXXIV, No. 1, March 1960.

along; that is, how 'the family' is meeting the appropriate needs of its individual parts for the purpose of sustaining and developing patterns for life.

It is also our impression that treatment methodology and skills necessary to carry out the goals set by a family diagnosis within this context would not require basic modification of the equipment of the experienced worker. We wish to add quickly, however, that this last impression may not hold up with the accumulation of further knowledge and experience.

In the first place, we have found that it is essential to family diagnosis, as we understand it, to begin by establishing a point of view about the family as a functioning and interacting entity which provides the major setting for the ego development or ego functioning of each member. This is not as easy as it may sound. Our whole discipline of understanding human beings has been related to the individual. We have reached out to appreciate some of the positive and negative values of interpersonal reactions, and we give recognition to these in our work with clients. Such 'interpersonal reactions' are inevitably evaluated in terms of how A affects B and in turn affects C.

Too often, however, as we talk about family diagnosis, we immediately move into the detailed consideration of the separate parts. This is like trying to understand the functions of a molecule entirely by a study of its particles. Although the particles have function and value in themselves and contribute to the molecular structure, there is a whole area of dynamic function that belongs to the molecule as a unit that provides a meaning to the particle. The same can very well be said of the family, but as a profession we have to develop a real conviction that such a specific function is carried out by 'the family' on which the individuals making up the group are dependent. It goes without saying that the individuals, in turn, react on 'the family' and its function. But, in order to understand the function of 'the family' we are in need of knowledge and skills in addition to those we have traditionally employed in looking at individuals and their interaction.

For our purposes we have been leaning heavily on the dynamic concept of family function suggested somewhat separately by Parsons[1] and by Pollak in an early paper on a suggested model of a family.[2]

[1] Talcott Parsons, Robert F. Bales, and Collaborators, *Family, Socialization and Interaction Process*, Free Press, Glencoe, Ill., 1955.

[2] Otto Pollak, 'Family Situations and Child Development', *Children*, Vol. IV, September-October, 1957, 169-73.

These concepts are that the main functions of a 'family' are the satisfaction of the major emotional requirements of the adults in the family and the appropriate preparation of children to handle the requirements of life. We have found this concept more workable than the often-found descriptions of family functions as shelter, protection, and socialization, which can easily become sterile. Such an approach also recognizes a dynamic force that also shapes the individual's functioning and adjustment and gives us a better understanding of personality patterns than just a description of the person's internal needs and how these have been met. This force, for want of a better term, may be called the value system that a person absorbs through the opinions, attitudes, and concepts to which he is exposed and which become firmly integrated in the ego as well as the superego structure.

We recognize the need for more specific knowledge about the structure, dynamics, and functions of 'the family' which might be pulled together from our unconceptualized professional experience as well as from other related disciplines. To search through other literature can easily become a bewildering experience for a person without enough background, particularly in relation to the work of some of the other disciplines. There is a great need for real communication between fields. Some material may easily sound highly theoretical or may even appear to clash openly with what we know from our own experience. We have had to move slowly and cautiously in evaluating what and how much of this 'other field' knowledge we can use at this time. We are not entirely sure, for example, that we are able to differentiate soundly between the theory of role interaction and the theory of dynamic processes that go on between the individuals in a family. There seems to be validity, but probably a great deal of overlapping, in the theories. We also hear about the communication processes that go on in the family and all the implications they hold for family members. We have been more traditionally exposed to the cultural values that come to bear on a family group, although formal conceptualization has often been too limited to nationality differences. We are also aware that there are studies of leadership roles in the family—of who makes what decision, how leadership changes hands, and how this change affects family interaction. Finally, there are value constellations in the community that cut across family concepts and processes, providing support, creating tension, or bringing change in family attitudes and patterns.

It is quite possible that if the various social sciences were to communicate comfortably and clearly with one another, we might together conceptualize the common major principles that would be of great value to us all. We might also find, perhaps, because of the volume of accumulated experience in practice, that there is less newness about these basic principles than might be supposed.

In order to begin to develop something that could be utilized in practice, we had to choose where to start and what tools to use in evaluating a specific family. For this, our staff has found a very useful tool in a methodology suggested by Pollak in a seminar at our agency. This frame of reference might be listed as (a) the membership and structure of the family, (b) the functions of the sub-systems in the family, (c) the relationship tendencies, (d) the functional performance of the family members, and (e) the individual dynamics of the members. Each of these elements will be considered separately.

The membership and structure of the family. In considering the over-all structure of a family, we are trying to define the skeletal frame to which the individuals are attached. For example: Is it complete in terms of parents and children? Are both sexes represented in the sibling group? Is the age-span of the children such that continuity of development—physical, emotional, and social—can be meaningful to them? Has anyone died or dropped out along the way? Another part of this consideration is the rigidity or flexibility of the basic skeleton. Is it tough, resilient, and able to take shock, or brittle, or functioning behind a façade? Does it serve as a pipe-line from generation to generation, passing on concepts, values, and attitudes, or is there feeling of discontinuity?

Functions of the sub systems within the family. Within this skeletal structure our next step is to examine the functions of the sub systems. These are in effect sub structures organized around definite functions drawing certain family members together at certain times. Basically, we have been using three sub systems: spouse, parent-child, and sibling. Some of our families, however, include one or more grandparents and some include a relative, either a child or adult, or an outside child such as a foster child. These additions often seem to set up other sub structures which at times activate positive and/or negative values for the family as a group; but these preliminary impressions need further study.

In each of these sub systems we try to determine what is going on. In the spouse system, we are concerned with whether the husband and wife are usually meeting each other's major emotional needs. Are the adults obtaining from each other most of the emotional satisfaction they require? In the parent-child system, we are concerned with the function of communicating values and gratifying needs in order to allow and promote adequate ego growth of the child. In the sibling system we look, for example, to see if it is possible at this level for the child to make trial solutions of problems of development before taking on the adults (e.g. testing out rivalries with parents on siblings first). We consider the positive support and guidance that may be passed on from an older sibling to a younger sibling or the gratification in growth that may be experienced by an older sibling through helping a younger sibling.

The relationship tendencies. Our third step is to examine the relationship tendencies in the home. Here we are concerned about whether or not the individuals as units belong to the whole. Does the skeletal structure serve as a magnet, a fortress, a prison, or a force that drives the units outward to scatter them as soon as feasible? Is the natural 'pairing' that occurs at certain developmental stages prolonged inappropriately? Is there a ganging-up or freezing-out process affecting some member of the group? The family climate will have very different effects on the various members.

The functional performance of the family members. In looking at functional performance, we have focused primarily on the dynamic roles of family members. Here we are using 'role' to mean the expectation of behaviour or attitude that a person has for himself in a given setting or situation while at the same time he expects someone else to respond to him. If the 'other' person responds as expected by the originator of the role, there is functional complementarity. For example, if a husband sees his role as returning home at the end of a day as a tired breadwinner in need of peace and rest and his wife sees her role as welcoming the tired toiler with a drink, an easy chair, and no responsibilities, there is complementarity. If the other person has a different expectation and reacts accordingly, there is dysfunction between the two, which then produces disequilibrium. The role that an individual expects of himself, and for which he expects a complementary reaction, no doubt is related to some kind of combination between his set of values and his internal needs. Just what this relationship is requires much more study and examination. However, we believe that the individual assumes more meaning if we see his functioning as related at least to these two forces.

The psychological dynamics of the individual. The final area of consideration is, of course, familiar to all family caseworkers, namely, the individual dynamics of a family member—how well he has been able to integrate his various needs and his ego development. Historical

APPLYING FAMILY DIAGNOSIS IN PRACTICE 173

material, as well as present functioning, will be included in such an assessment.

The third major area of consideration, i.e. the application of our established skills of exploration and evaluation to the family as a whole, is directed towards identifying those bench marks which will tell us how it is going with a particular family and the individuals within it. The disciplined skills in diagnosing an individual have made it possible for a caseworker, in an exceedingly brief period of time compared to a person's total existence, to gain a fairly accurate impression about where a person is in his development. Considerable experience will undoubtedly be needed before we have the same skill in really evaluating a family.

The frame of reference just described so briefly appears to give us a workable assessment of what is right, and what is wrong, with the family, but any treatment plan must be directed to individuals. Hence we must have an additional perspective. To obtain this we ask these questions: What are the important role operations of the individual, whether originated by him or required by some other member's role? Do any of these major roles disrupt the other individual's personality or defence system in a significant way? How much do these major roles support or disrupt the originating individual's total personality? Does the role satisfy the person's needs to a major extent? Is there some dissatisfaction or lack of gratification left over in spite of what he has done? Or is there a real disruption of a significant part of the total personality?

These questions need considerable elaboration. We do believe a role may gratify a specific need of the person and yet place great stress on other parts of the personality. We also believe that this depth inspection of a role—i.e. examining its effect on the person internally in relation to gratification and the effect on defence structures—is necessary to give validity to looking at roles as a way of determining a therapeutic aim.

Effect of major role on other persons. It has been said in other places, but perhaps not often enough realized in our field, that the force of the value system is indeed powerful. We can see that certain things that a person expects of himself, or that are expected of him by others, can openly clash with certain internal needs of that individual. This clash can even reach the point of causing considerable tension or disruption. At other times the value systems can play a very important role in determining the actual pattern used to express a personality defence. We are all familiar with the person who basically has a very passive orientation to life, yet, in order to meet the expectation of either his primary group or society at large will overlay this with a very aggressive façade, which, while uncomfortable and threatening, has tremendous significance to the person's self-esteem and will be bitterly defended.

In examining the dynamic concept of role—i.e. the interaction of the expectancy of what 'I think, do, or wish for myself' and a complementing act, wish or attitude of someone else—we realize that we are dealing with a situation that is never static, never isolated. Spiegel[1] has pointed out, for example, that there is almost a chronic need to establish equilibrium as each role situation gives way to the next. The situation becomes even more complex if an individual is maintaining a number of specific roles. Some roles the individual may be originating, some may be complementary roles to somebody else's expectation. It would be virtually impossible to try to catalogue all the roles or all that they mean. We have attempted, however, to try to pull out what may be the more significant groups of roles in family life. We have identified five general role areas that we think give us a cross-section of general important functioning between husband and wife. These five relate to emotional gratification, economic functions, home maintenance, family ideal (i.e. the hopes and aspirations and ultimate goals for the group), and the breadwinning function. For the other major role areas we consider the respective roles in parent-child relationships, the roles between siblings, and the family roles of the male sex and the female sex. Further experience might well modify this arbitrary selection of major role areas.

Once we identify the functional problems appearing in the roles in these various major areas, we differentiate whether the difficulty arises primarily from interpersonal or intrapsychic causes. In the interpersonal area, we look at the friction points to determine more specifically where the functional problem lies. Is this, for example, a conflict in role concepts growing out of one member's values and expectancies that are not being complemented by the other important person? Or is the clash in the interaction between personality needs of the persons involved? Or does dysfunction occur because one person's role disrupts the other person's personality in general or defence structure in particular?

An example of a clash between role (and value) concepts would be too obvious to require space in this paper. However, it is important

[1] John P. Spiegel, 'The Resolution of Role Conflict within the Family', *Psychiatry*, Vol. XX, February 1957, 1-16.

to note that resolution of such a conflict is not always a simple matter of education or compromise. When the values involved are deeply imbedded in the ego structure and operate for the most part automatically, they are not easily conceptualized or modified. Probably the same consideration is necessary as in changing any other part of ego structure. A strictly intellectual attempt of the client to override a deeply integrated value system will result in some degree of chronic tension or anxiety or may augment fears that have been held in delicate balance by a defence mechanism.

As an example of a situation in which the interaction dysfunction in the conflict lay between one person's role and another person's defence, we have a mother, who in her sense of values conceives the mother's role as nurturing, protecting, and caring for her very young children. In her particular social group, this is a responsibility that is expected to be shared by the father. Her husband, however, because of his own life-experience came into the marriage with much repressed dependency which he has handled by a very rigorous, independent approach to his education, occupation (draughtsman), and social relationships. He is close to his wife. His need for her meets emotional requirements as a fairly dependent person who wants to be needed. Also, in other ways their roles tend to support each other in general, in that both want a 'close' type of family life, involving mutual planning, and one tends to include the other in arriving at decisions. However, in the particular area of child care, his wife's concept of the parent's role as being protective, giving, and almost standing between the children and the requirements of life is becoming extremely threatening to this young man's defences against his own dependency. As a complement to her role she expects him to do much the same thing that she does with the children. However, he is unable to carry out this role without becoming extremely anxious and then breaking down into verbal attack or storming out of the house. He is certain that his children are being raised as a group of cissies who will not be able to survive.

In looking at this situation we used some of our concepts in considering how pressure in the family might be alleviated without deep therapy for the young father, something which was neither economically nor emotionally possible for this family. Some modification was apparently made here as the worker began to separate the wife's role expectancy from the husband's. Although relieving the husband of what had been earlier expected of him by his wife does not change the underlying picture of his difficulties, there has been a substantial

difference in the tone in the family and there has been some benefit
to the children. Through a deliberate process the role expectancies
were modified. Encouragement was given to the wife in developing a
role expectancy of the father which would play in somewhat with his
wish to convey to the children some of the independence which was
so important to him. Some fairly direct interpretation with the mother
helped to relieve her of including her husband in the role she saw
herself playing. At the same time, fairly direct interpretation to the
father of the stages of development of children did modify his focus
on independence without regard to the children's stages of development.

We did not propose for a minute that this is a new kind of work.
It has been going on in family casework to some degree for a very
long time. However, too often it is the kind of undisciplined use of
experience and hunches on the part of the skilled worker that brings
about such solutions. It is our hope that by bringing such a frame of
reference into focus workers will be able, when appropriate, to effect
such approaches more quickly than they might when forced to depend
solely upon whatever it is that brings professional hunches into
operation.

Effect of major role on originating person. An extremely important
part of this consideration of roles, however, is the effect of the role
of a person, whether originating with him or with someone else, on
his own intrapsychic structure. This perhaps is the real key which
gives us a smooth transition from individual dynamics to family
functioning and expectancies. A role may be generally compatible
with the intrapsychic pattern but still may not satisfy inner needs.
The gap between what the role supports and the total need will
produce a feeling of a lack of fulfilment and will cause tension or
increasing anxiety.

For example, it is not uncommon for a family agency to have
applications, and periodic reapplications, from 'suffering spouses'
whose masochistic drives have led them into personally distressing
marriages. Such persons are subject to a periodic increase of anxiety
and come in to complain about their partners and the life they have
to lead, indirectly debasing themselves further. They have little
motivation to change, yet something is wrong. What is wrong with
their balance in the marriage will depend on the situation. Perhaps for
some the degree of self-punishment achieved by their life-situation,
while compatible to a substantial part of their personality organization,
just is not enough. Consequently, to the degree that the role they

achieve does not meet their inner requirements, anxiety begins to accumulate. At some point the client then has to find a release for this tension and this, rather than a real desire for any change in living pattern, is the real motivation for their coming to the agency.

On the other hand, we also find that an important role may be frictional or seriously disruptive to the individual's intrapsychic structure. Take, for example, the young, highly intellectual Steehls. Mr Steehl is a technical engineer responsible for the work of several assistants. The family lives in a middle-class neighbourhood, semi-isolated from neighbours, and only vaguely in contact with a peer group of engineers and scientists. Mrs Steehl is basically a hostile person who is very competitive with men and whose bitter cross in life is that she is a female and unable to be a leading scientist. Yet her role is in sharp contrast with her wish. She has driven hard at adopting the role of a socially acceptable housewife and mother. In her four years of marriage she has studied Spock, Gesell, budget manuals, and housekeeping journals. Her mounting anger is loading her with anxiety that approaches real panic. In carrying out her household responsibilities, she is doing only the minimum. One gets the impression of an ego structure that is breaking down.

Mr Steehl is not yet so badly damaged, but he appears to be heading in the same direction. Basically a passive, dependent person, he has taken on the values of his father and family as to the masculine role. He must hold a respected position; he must make responsible decisions; he must be competively aggressive; he must be boss. So far, he has attained this, but in the three years since entering employment he has also acquired colitis symptoms that at times incapacitate him.

Both adults are pushing to their limits to sustain roles that clash directly with their internal structure, yet both are unable to give up these roles that are so important to their defence and self-esteem. Very intensive individual treatment is needed here if a serious break-down is to be forestalled.

More time and more examination will be needed to understand fully the complex relationship between role assumption, the value system, and the inner dynamics of the individual. Although our profession has long had deep convictions about the intrapsychic forces and about the historical effect of life-experiences in shaping the personality, such convictions have, at times, not provided the caseworker with a workable approach to a client. It is our belief that, by using a wider scheme that includes the value system of the individual as well as his functioning in major role areas, we can move quickly to deter-

M

mine the strengths and weaknesses and the areas in which they operate. In experience we find that the positives are much more readily available than the negatives and that they give us a more sure idea of what we want to begin with in treatment.

Actually, this paper is an interim report on the application of family diagnosis in a family agency. There is need for a great deal of experience, testing-out, and mutual communication with allied professional fields in order to clarify and implement concepts which now seem strange and cumbersome. But our experience leaves us with the firm conviction that as we move in this direction our capacity to understand and to be of help will be greatly enriched.

15

DESIGNING AN INSTRUMENT TO ASSESS PARENTAL COPING MECHANISMS*

JACOB I. HURWITZ, PH.D.

DAVID M. KAPLAN, PH.D.

ELIZABETH KAISER

AMONG the proposed approaches for curbing delinquent behaviour in children is the modification of disruptive parent-child relationship patterns. Before such patterns can be modified, however, effective methods of assessing them must be devised. To be fully adequate these methods must distinguish between constructive and disruptive parent-child relationship patterns in a manner that will provide clear blueprints for remedial action.

This article describes an attempt to devise a measurement tool to make such an assessment of parental coping mechanisms. Made within the context of an extensive multidisciplinary delinquency research project, the endeavour, carried out at the South Shore Guidance Centre, combined clinical social work methods with quantitative research techniques.

The theory underlying this part of the overall study is based largely on the concepts of Erich Lindemann and Gerald Caplan concerning crisis situations and David M. Kaplan's related concept of acute situational disorders. According to their formulations, when an acute, stress-producing situation, or crisis, occurs in a family—for example, the death of a family member—the manner in which the family members respond to the situation and cope with it is a matter of considerable theoretical and practical importance. They postulate that for each major type of acute situational disorder there is a specific set of psychological tasks—for example, 'grief work'—that must be accomplished if the situational problem is to be successfully resolved. If these tasks are not

* Published in Social Casework, Vol. XLIII, No. 10, December 1962.

accomplished, the acute situational disorder can generate chronic intra-psychic or social maladjustment.

In the study reported here, this conceptual framework was applied to the problem of juvenile delinquency, and an effort was made to specify some of the psychological tasks that parents of court delinquents must accomplish if the acute disorder is not to become chronic —that is to say, if recidivism is to be prevented. The view was taken that each family of a court delinquent goes through a crisis created by the court summons and that this experience is a painful and upsetting one to most families, although in different degrees and perhaps for different reasons. The results of a pilot study had suggested that there is only a limited number of ways in which parents generally respond to this crisis and handle it with each other, with the delinquent boy, and with the court. It was recognized, of course, that the family's functioning at such a time may differ somewhat from its usual behaviour, but it was believed that parental responses to the crisis situation should provide clues to the family's basic structure, its strengths, and its weaknesses. The initial plan had been to make a conventional assessment of family structure. This was impossible, however, because members of the social work team were limited to a single interview in which to gather data for the project psychiatrist on the juvenile offender's social developmental history and the context of the offence. It was decided, therefore, to focus on current parental mechanisms as being of equal theoretical relevance, a more feasible approach practically, and more useful for control purposes.

The project staff postulated that it should be possible by focusing on how the parents responded to the delinquent act, to make a family diagnosis that would lead directly to a constructive treatment plan for the family. Such an outcome could be expected because factors to be assessed are those that bear directly on current parent-child relations, about which something can be done. For example, if the kind of plan the parents make for the boy as a result of the court experience is deemed ineffectual in preventing further delinquent behaviour, or actually likely to encourage it, it is open to modification.

Most families who are sent by the Court to the South Shore Guidance Centre are not highly motivated to accept clinical treatment, and many are inaccessible. The project staff believed, however, that the family diagnosis resulting from the clinic's study and evaluation would make it possible to spot trouble areas and that a quite direct approach to the parents, frequently on a short-term basis, might help them to modify some of their coping patterns. A joint treatment plan, a kind of milieu therapy, was thus envisaged, in which direct social work intervention with the family would supplement some type of intervention with the boy. Such a plan is not appropriate for all families. It works best with those parents who fall within the upper range of emotional health. These are the parents who are likely to make progress on their own after a brief series of interviews. This same approach may be used in a more limited way with certain more disturbed families; they can be pulled through the crisis and encouraged to return to the clinic for further clinical intervention.

To facilitate making a family diagnosis, a rating schedule was devised by a team of four experienced psychiatric social workers operating under the technical direction of the senior author, a research specialist. The reason for this approach to the task of devising the schedule was to avoid imposing upon the social work raters an alien, custom-made measurement model, to make maximum use of the professional judgment and clinical competence of the social work team in devising the instrument, not merely in using it. The basic strategy was to make the tool-building process a joint collaborative effort in which the knowledge and skills of social practice and of social research could be productively integrated.

This strategy was implemented in several ways. First, the social work team decided, as was explained earlier, to focus on current parental responses to the delinquent act, rather than on prior family structure, for the purpose of getting a measure of family coping mechanisms. The team then analysed records of court cases interviewed during the previous year to isolate the nature and range of parental responses to the delinquent crisis. After a series of model responses had been selected and refined, several measurement models were tested until an appropriate one was found. The major criteria applied in assessing appropriateness were ease in rating and in interpretation, reliability and validity of ratings, and quantifiability of clinical interview material to permit its statistical manipulation.

The rating schedule does not focus on the personality structure of the parents or the child, but on some interpersonal factors perceived as potential determinants of the delinquent child's future behaviour— which are therefore promising targets in a delinquency control programme.

After a considerable amount of trial-and-error experimentation,*

* Research design in all its phases is rarely the neat, orderly, and sure-footed process that it appears to be from a reading of most research reports. When social practitioners and social researchers attempt to combine creatively their respective bodies of knowledge

five general areas of parental coping were selected for empirical study:

1. Parent-to-child communication.
2. Parent-to-parent communication.
3. Parent-to-court communication.
4. Parental assessment of the problem.
5. The parental remedial action plan.

The specific behaviours tapped by the schedule are these:

1. The nature and quality of parent-child and parent-parent communications in relation to the crisis situation.
2. The parents' views on what particular problems are responsible for the delinquent act.
3. Their choice of problem areas on which to focus their respective action plans.
4. The nature of the action plan directed towards the child.
5. The kind of help they want from the court.

The schedule is structured in terms of a rough sequence of parental behaviours considered necessary—though not by themselves sufficient —to deter delinquency. Its function is to permit an *assessment* of the *degree* to which, and the *areas* within which, parental coping mechanisms in this situation are adaptive or maladaptive in delinquency control.

Adaptive coping on the part of parents is conceptualized as the parents' seeing the child's need for help, showing a capacity for self-involvement, formulating and carrying out a constructive action plan, communicating effectively with the child and with each other, and using the court constructively. The following abbreviated summary is an illustration of typical parental adaptive coping mechanisms:

Mrs K talked seriously to Walter about what he had done. Walter told his mother that he resented the many restrictions put on him because of his poor school work and felt he could not achieve the standard his parents set. Mrs K does feel that some blame should be placed on Walter for his attitude. On the other hand, she feels that the neighbourhood environment makes it hard for a boy to be interested in academic achievement and that she has not taken time to listen to and understand her son. Mrs K plans to get him some

---

and skill to carry out a piece of research, the process necessarily entails even more floundering than usual. Thus, for example, a high level of frustration tolerance is probably as essential in *studying* delinquent behaviour as in *curbing* it.

tutorial help if he can use it. She has also talked with her husband, and they have agreed that they will both try to put less emphasis on school performance.

Mrs K thinks that the court hearing served a useful purpose. Though she thinks she can manage without further help, she sees the probation officer as someone who could help her if the need arose.

Mr K also talked with his son. Since he already knew from Mrs K how Walter felt, he raised the issues that concerned Walter and offered to try to see the boy's side of the problem and to make some changes. Mr K agrees with what his wife said about Walter and the neighbourhood. He also recognizes that education is important to him and that he is angry with his son for not doing well in school.

Mr K and his wife discussed the problem, and Mr K agreed to support Mrs K's plan. The communication between the parents was strengthened by this crisis. For a few years Mr K had been so engrossed in his business that he had taken little time to talk to his wife. They now realized how much they missed their earlier discussions.

Maladaptive coping is defined as the parents' denying the delinquent act, despite official verification; projecting responsibility on to the child, on to bad environmental influences, or on to the other parent; or seeing the court appearance as an unwarranted intrusion into their lives. An illustration of typical maladaptive coping mechanism follows:

Mrs T tried to confront Bert with the delinquent act, but in a very half-hearted and cursory fashion, since she has no relationship with him. As a result, no serious discussion between mother and child took place. She blames Bert and his friends for his getting into trouble and does not consider herself in any way responsible for the act.

Mrs T thinks it is useless to do anything about the boy's delinquent act because she feels she cannot carry out a plan. She thinks anything she tries to do will be futile. Mrs T wants the court to take over and not involve her. It is all right with her if they wish to take Bert away from home.

Mr T did not come for the interview. Mrs T thinks he feels much as she does about the boy. However, she cannot talk to her husband and therefore is not sure.

The parents of each court delinquent were given an interview of about an hour and a half, first together and then individually. The joint session was held to observe their interaction patterns and to get basic data on parental coping mechanisms. The individual sessions were used to supplement and validate these data in a somewhat freer atmosphere. The interview with the mother was also used to elicit the social-developmental data required by the psychiatrist.

Each set of parents was rated by the examining social worker immediately after the interview. A statistical clerk computed assessment scores for the mother and for the father in each of the five specific areas of parental coping listed above. These scores ranged from *very constructive* to *constructive*, to *destructive* to *very destructive*. Thus, for example, an earnest and serious two-way discussion of the delinquent act between a parent and the child was assessed as *very constructive* parent-child communication; a one-way discussion, earnest and serious on the parent's part but with little participation by the boy, was assessed as *constructive* communication; a token parental confrontation of the boy was assessed as *destructive*; and no discussion at all as *very destructive*. Overall paternal and maternal coping scores were derived by summating the five area assessments, assigning a weight of three to the type of action plan envisaged, since it was considered the most crucial factor in deterring further delinquency. Overall family coping scores were then derived by combining the father's and mother's overall coping scores with a measure of their congruence.

Figure 1 presents the formula for deriving these family coping scores.

FIGURE 1

FORMULA FOR DERIVING: OVERALL FAMILY COPING SCORES

Parental Coping Score	Overall Family Coping Score
Father ++ or ++ or + Mother ++ or + or ++	= ++ very constructive
Father + or ++ or − Mother + or − or ++	= + constructive
Father + or − or − or ++ or −− Mother − or + or − or −− or ++	= − destructive
Father + or −− or − or −− or −− Mother −− or + or −− or − or −−	= −− very destructive

The formula was evolved as a result of the repeated difficulties encountered in trying to achieve satisfactory interrater reliability on high-level inferences. It was decided to modify conventional practice by using highly experienced psychiatric social workers to rate factual items and low-level inferences but not to rate the crucial high-level inferences. The problem of avoiding the rating of high-level inferences was solved by getting a consensus on the criteria for deriving these inferences from the descriptive ratings.

When thoroughly mastered, the instrument can be rated in less than ten minutes. As new workers were trained by the same process that had been used in testing for reliability, the use of the instrument was found to be easy to teach. It can be readily used by non clinical personnel, such as probation officers, with the help of a good operational manual. This is true because, as stated earlier, the high-level inferences are made with the help of formulae that can be applied with nothing more than good clerical skill.

Since the focus of this schedule is on current behavioural data, reliability was easier to achieve than for schedules whose items require the rating of clinical inferences. Items were operationally defined in a rating manual where necessary, but many items were defined on the rating schedule itself.

The schedule went through three major revisions. Before each revision, a pre-test was conducted on ten to twelve cases, each rated by three or four raters. The final schedule was tested for reliability on twenty cases. During this formal reliability test the social workers interviewed in rotation, and were observed by two or three other social workers through a one-way screen. The schedule was rated by both interviewer and observer. Reliability conferences were held after each interview (as they had been on previous pre-tests), and ambiguous items were operationally defined Items that remained unreliable were either revised or deleted. Good reliability* was achieved on most items.

The first draft of the schedule was structured mainly in the form of dichotomous items calling for statements about the presence or absence of various attitudes or behaviour. Owing to the difficulties encountered in trying to rate these items reliably, many of them were opened up into seven-point scales requiring rather sophisticated clinical inferences. The team soon discovered, however, that the interview did not provide an adequate observational basis for rating some of these

* Good reliability is here defined as agreement at the ·05 level of significance as determined by chi-square test.

items with any degree of subjective confidence or objective reliability. At this point it was decided to eliminate unrateable inferential items from the schedule, to replace them by essentially factual dichotomous items or three- to four-point ordinal scales, and to derive the basic clinical assessment items objectively by predetermined formulae from the pattern of responses to the factual items.

For example, an unrateable inferential item, such as 'How adequate was the mother's (father's) diagnosis?' structured as a seven-point ordinal scale ranging from *highly adequate* to *highly inadequate*, was converted into a series of dichotomous factual ratings, such as 'In discussing the causes of the delinquent act, where does the mother (father) locate the problem(s)':

(a) Outside the family?	Yes	No
(b) In the child?	Yes	No
(c) In the self?	Yes	No

Since the thirty-seven ratings called for by the schedule are all descriptive rather than inferential in nature, item reliability levels were, of course, quite high. For the same reason considerable confidence can be placed in the accuracy of the behavioural data yielded by the instrument. Since, however, the crucial assessments of parental handling were derived from predetermined formulae based on clinical judgment, their validity requires empirical verification.

The factors differentiating delinquents coming from families who coped constructively with the court crisis from those who coped destructively with it were examined for evidence relating to the validity of assessing parental coping patterns as a major factor in delinquency. The latter cases more often showed evidences of social maladjustment and emotional disturbance than did the former. This was manifested by such characteristics among the delinquents as a history of developmental difficulties, recent major failure experiences, overtly aggressive delinquent acts, an absence of feelings of guilt, a disruptive attitude towards the diagnostic group, and the high level of psychopathology of the offenders and their mothers. All these factors differentiated constructive from destructive parental coping mechanisms more sharply than they did high- from low-delinquency areas of residence. These factors, therefore, cannot be attributed solely (or perhaps even primarily) to sociocultural influences.

The findings suggest that the assessment of parental coping mechanisms is a valid diagnostic procedure. They further suggest that current parental coping mechanisms may reflect earlier child-rearing patterns, and so reflect stable and persisting aspects of family structure.

This article has described an attempt made, in the context of a wider study, to devise a tool for assessing parent-child relationship patterns in a manner that will provide clear blueprints for remedial action. The related concepts of crisis situation and acute situational disorder were applied to the delinquency situation, and an effort was made to specify some of the coping mechanisms parents of court delinquents must use in order to help prevent the acute disorder brought on by the court experience from becoming chronic. It was postulated that, by focusing on how the parents responded to the delinquent act, it should be possible to make a family diagnosis that could lead directly to a constructive and frequently short-term, treatment plan for the family.

The tool-building process was set up as a collaborative effort between researcher and practitioners to exploit to the full the clinical knowledge of the social work team in devising the measurement instrument, not merely in using it. The instrument that was devised is designed to tap the parents' assessment of the court crisis and their actions to prevent recurrences. Its function is to assess, within selected areas, the degree to which parental coping mechanisms are adaptive or maladaptive for purposes of delinquency control. Adaptive and maladaptive coping mechanisms were conceptually and operationally defined.

In this presentation, the data-gathering, rating and assessment processes have been described in some detail, the formula for deriving assessments of family coping patterns has been presented, and the rateability of the instrument and its use by personnel not clinically trained have been discussed. The methodological procedures utilized to refine and standardize the instrument have been reviewed, and evidence concerning its reliability and validity presented. In conclusion, it has been asserted that parental coping mechanisms in this crisis situation appear, in general, to reflect stable and persisting aspects of family structure.

THE END

GEORGE ALLEN & UNWIN LTD

London: 40 Museum Street, W.C.1

Auckland: 24 Wyndham Street
Bombay: 15 Graham Road, Ballard Estate, Bombay 1
Bridgetown: P.O. Box 222
Buenos Aires: Escritorio 454-459, Florida 165
Calcutta: 17 Chittaranjan Avenue, Calcutta 13
Cape Town: 68 Shortmarket Street
Hong Kong: 44 Mody Road, Kowloon
Ibadan: P.O. Box 62
Karachi: Karachi Chambers, McLeod Road
Madras: Mohan Mansions, 38c Mount Road, Madras 6
Mexico: Villalongin 32-10, Piso, Mexico 5, D.F.
Nairobi: P.O. Box 4536
New Delhi: 13-15 Asaf Ali Road, New Delhi 1
Ontario: 81 Curlew Drive, Don Mills
Philippines: 7 Waling-Waling Street, Roxas District, Quezon City
São Paulo: Caixa Postal 8675
Singapore: 36c Prinsep Street, Singapore 7
Sydney, N.S.W.: Bradbury House, 55 York Street
Tokyo: 10 Kanda-Ogawamachi, 3-Chome, Chiyoda-Ku